PERSUASION SKILLS

HOW TO LEARN ALL TECHNIQUES OF THE ART OF PERSUASION, IMPROVE YOUR SKILLS, UNDERSTAND PSYCHOLOGY AND INFLUENCE PEOPLE.

John Austin

Published by Mybook Self-Publishing Ltd

Table of Contents

Introduction

In life, anywhere you look, there are chances to be persuaded. Whether it is the billboard you pass on your way to work, the person you text most often, or even the lover with whom you share children, these things and people can be influential and persuasive. You may have already identified obvious forms of persuasion, and maybe that is how you landed on this book. While it is important to know how others may be influencing you, it is an entirely different concept to figure out how to influence others.

Persuasion and influence are an art, and like art, they take practice. After you have completed this reading, you will better understand persuasion. However, you may not be able to go out and convince everyone of what you want them to do right away. It takes time, but if you stay committed to your goals and dedicated to your intentions, you will become a master persuader in no time.

The aim of persuasion is not to manipulate but to bring people to decisions that are in their best interest and to help further worthwhile causes. These are causes that are beneficial and bring value to society. While you will most likely benefit from the persuasion tactics in which you choose to partake, you should ensure that they are beneficial for other parties involved as well.

If you continue to take from people but never give back, this behavior may haunt you one day. Persuasion and influence should be viewed in a positive light as tools that help people, not as a means of hurting others.

The foundation for the practice of influence and persuasion is understanding human psychology, how people make decisions, and how they are wired. Everyone is different, so the ways that you decide to persuade them will differ as well. If you are knowledgeable about psychology, you will have an easier time differentiating individuals and understanding what persuasion tactics are best used on them.

From there, techniques and practices can be pursued sincerely. If you are genuine with intention and actually want to help people, it will be easy to adopt the methods and strategies of some excellent influencers and persuaders. Remember that it is going to take some trial and error, and not everyone will agree with your viewpoint right away. Make sure that you are in a mindset where you are ready to take criticism and willing to accept the fact that some people just will not be persuaded.

Learning starts by making sure that you are aware of the power of influence and persuasion. They can be harmful tools if they are put into the wrong hands, and as you are reading these words, a few people probably come to mind right away. In order to ensure that you are not using these methods of influence improperly, we are going to take you through negative stereotypes to ensure that you are not someone who is going to take advantage of anyone.

When used correctly, persuasion and influence can elicit positive change in groups of people rather than just from individual to individual. Connecting with people on a general level and determining mutual interests will be helpful in ensuring you are someone who can easily persuade others.

When you understand that these methods can be very helpful in your life, you can start to learn ways in which you can implement the best practices into your everyday activity. There are many benefits and advantages to being a persuasive person. The most obvious one is that you will be better at getting what you want.

From there, you will realize that you have more confidence, which can seriously reduce stress and anxiety. By reducing these things alone, you are going to feel much better; you will have the power needed to be the person you have always wanted to be.

It is important to know the difference between influence and persuasion. They are related, and you cannot have one without the other. However, the terms are not interchangeable. One means a specific moment, and the other is in reference to a more prolonged period of encouragement. This book will lay the groundwork and understandings of each so you can create your own personalized methods of persuasion and influence to help you achieve the goals you may have been ignoring.

Once you learn how to be persuasive, you will most likely be happier altogether. Instead of sitting silently in the background, you will be able to use your voice to speak up for what matters. Though it might seem scary at times, you are going to become the person you have always admired; an influential and inspirational leader who knows what it takes to be successful. Your confidence will keep building over time, especially the more you practice refining your skills.

Examples are provided, but remember to apply the methods and techniques specifically to your situation. We are all different, and our levels of expertise differ as well. You will be confronting those you wish to persuade, so ensure that you are personalizing your strategies to your individual life. That is what being a persuasive influencer is all about!

Chapter 1 Principles Of Persuasion

When we discuss manipulation and persuasion, it usually comes down to a difference of intent. For instance, is the person who is persuading you to do something that will benefit both you and them? If so, that's the classic win-win scenario, and we could say that persuasion was used to help you come to the right decision.

But what if the same person gets you to do something that benefits him, but leaves you worse off? That would be characterized as manipulation, and that type of persuasion happens all of the time, too. You may have done it yourself without really realizing it, and not felt too good about it afterward.

Persuasion can be used for all kinds of purposes, both good and evil. People can manipulate you into giving them your money, your time, your faith, your talent, and provide you with nothing in return. Or they can persuade you into giving of all of these things and leave you better off in the end. And sometimes, the lines aren't so clearly drawn.

What I will attempt to show you in this book is just how persuasion happens in various parts of your everyday life, how persuasion can be used to help you get what you want, and how to recognize persuasion techniques that are used on you. Ultimately, everyone makes their own decisions. By being aware of persuasion techniques, you can more successfully analyze your motivations and make sure that what you are doing benefits both you and others.

Today's Pervasive Persuasion

Persuasion is also an important topic today because we are contacted by more and more sophisticated methods of persuasion than ever before. Persuasion comes at us in all forms, at a velocity never even possible previously. I'm sure you can guess the cause of this increased persuasion. That's right! It's called The Internet.

Never before have people had direct access to the tools of mass communication. You can pick up your smartphone and start broadcasting live right now, with just a few clicks. You can start typing and send your views to millions of people around the world. Or you can post a picture of that adorable thing your cat just did to your partner to brighten their day at work. And all of the people you are reaching can get that information instantly because they probably have a smartphone or computer or screen nearby that they are looking at, and you have access to that network. This type of reach and access was unheard of only a decade or two ago. Today, this connection is commonplace and growing.

But do you ever take time to decide how the words and pictures that you consume play a part in what you think, or what the motives were behind sending them to you in the first place?

Much like a loaded gun in the hands of someone who doesn't know how to shoot, persuasion techniques can sometimes have unintended consequences that can be devastating. If you don't realize what the warning signs are, or how you can protect yourself from those consequences, and make sure you aren't unintentionally harming yourself.

The Principles of Persuasion

Since that book, many researchers have created experiments to test these theories with surprisingly consistent results. The bottom line is that we humans seem to be hard-wired to behave in certain ways given certain circumstances. Using various methods to trigger those responses that we want, we can cause the outcomes that we want.

The 6 Principles Of Persuasion

Reciprocation

Give something to get something, right? Remember the story of the chicken who planted grain so that her chicks could eat? She asked for help to sow the grain, to keep the field clean from weeds, to harvest the grain and finally, to make the bread. She asked her neighbors and friends to help, but in the end, no one was interested until the bread was hot and ready to eat. Since her neighbors had not given her anything in the form of help, she was not inclined to give them any of the final product.

That give and take is the first principal of getting along in life, and it's known as one of the foundational principals of persuasion as well. Reciprocity merely means that if you give someone something, they are more likely to give you something in return.

Commitment and Consistency

We, humans, have a "reality" surrounding us at all times. I put this "reality" in quotes because it is a reality of our creation.

Our brains have an innate ability to tell stories, and we tell ourselves stories all of the time. We tell ourselves stories of the type of person we believe we are, and how we behave feeds into that story. When presented with a choice, you make that choice based on the story of who you are. One of the options looks "right" to us because making that choice is consistent with what we believe a person like us would do.

Social Proof

This core persuasion principle is also sometimes referred to as Consensus. Social proof feeds directly from the previous storytelling of Commitment and Consistency. We have told ourselves a story of what we believe we are, what we stand for, and the kind of person we are. To reinforce that story, we look at how other people behave for Social Proof of how people like us should react in a particular situation.

Now more than ever, the Internet has created countless places where we can go for this type of reinforcement. Some of that reinforcement is legitimate, some not so much. All of it is used as a powerful tool for persuasion, as we'll find out going forward.

Authority

Now once we have decided on the type of person we are and we've assembled with the kinds of people we believe reinforce that identity; the next step is to seek out knowledgeable people to reinforce what we've told ourselves to be true. That's where the idea of Authority takes hold.

As sane people, we are likely to take the advice of people who appear to have more knowledge about a subject than we do. That is certainly necessary. No one can know everything, not even with smartphones and Google just a tap away. We seek out the advice of people who know more about a subject than we do. We'll talk more about using this in persuasion later.

Liking

Liking is one of those core principles that seems obvious, but yet it needs definition since it is at the hub of all types of persuasion. Liking, simply put, means that you are much more likely to be persuaded by someone that you like.

If you don't like someone, are you going to take their advice? Probably not. We humans are wired to make snap judgments about almost every situation we get into, and one of the simplest decisions to make is whether we like someone or not. Every person you meet triggers a feeling instantly of comfort or wariness. This was a survival skill in the early days of our evolution, and it still holds sway today, as we'll see.

Scarcity

Speaking of evolution's early days, our final persuasion principal is an obvious holdover from the early days of staying alive. Scarcity makes things more valuable to us, so when something seems like it is limited in quantity, we are more likely to want it.

Sand is commonplace; gold is not. Which would you rather have? Or more to the point, what does all humankind want more? It most certainly used to be food that was so valuable, so that early man found ways to preserve food when it was abundant so that it would be around when food got scarce.

Survival depends on specific resources that can be in short supply, so humans are naturally prone to try and save and hang on to that which is not always available. Since this is core hardwiring in our brains, we'll see that this is an often-used method of persuasion today.

Chapter 2 Sales Persuasion

Selling constitutes the gist of all kinds of businesses. Though we often sell our point of views, professional selling involves selling of tangible or intangible products that may not be as simple as it may sound. Ask yourself a question – Would you buy something that you don't really need without giving it a second thought? Probably not; this is why if you want to be a successful sales person, you need to learn how to persuade and convince your prospects.

The Inner Game of Sales

Selling isn't merely about making the prospective buyer buy what he wants or what you may offer. It is also about making the buyer buy your perception about that service or product and start seeing it the way you have projected it. Selling is a mind game that needs to be first understood and then practiced. It relies on your belief that remains rested in your conscious as well as subconscious mind.

If we carry some sturdy opinion about the product or the service, and our mind believes in it, our selling power will get auto-empowered. For you to excel in sales, you ought to get a hold of your thoughts, ideas, and levels of concentration. Collect your mind and its ideas and pour it out in the form of conviction. This would set you on the right track and selling will start coming to you naturally.

Two important ingredients that would ensure you are making sales are positive attitude and prompt actions. Any delay in thinking or executing your plan would spoil the game.

Some strategic tips are:

There isn't any definite sales strategy that would become a benchmark for all.

Sales' skills need consistent honing for better results

The salesperson has to be smarter and rapt than the buyer to make him buy

Keep on innovating your strategies to not just sell your product but also prove it

Garner enough willingness, focus and concentration to excel in selling

How To Sell Without Losing Your Soul

Being a salesperson isn't easy. Even more difficult is to be an ethical salesperson who would sell without losing his or her soul. No one would believe a fake salesperson that puts on the charade of knowing you the moment they meet you. You would be shocked to know how the modern buyer is smart and knowledgeable.

So, instead of using your fake demeanor to sell, resort to some genuine counseling of your customer's need and sell the product out of his willingness. Believe in establishing a mutual and cordial relationship with your buyer without imposing yourself.

Here are some ways to be a likeable salesperson who believes in sane and rationale selling unlike those pushy ones who have gone redundant:

#1 Let Selling be not just Selling; solve a problem

The buyers are smart enough to gauge your mindset. They can sense if it is tilted towards hardcore selling or genuine for earning their loyalties. You don't have to focus on the word selling. Rather, take yourself as a guide who is going to help people in finding what they precisely need. This way, you would be able to understand the needs of your customers and appeal to their preferences.

#2 Do not be hell bent on selling

The harder you are trying to sell, the farther will your buyers be, out of distrust and doubt. Let the whole process of selling and buying be forgotten and lay stress on how you can help the customers. Trust me, it is going to show in your body language and you would end up being in the trusted books of your buyers. This would consequently help you in recommending your own product or service and customers will believe you easily.

If you want to be a successful sales person, you need to be honest and as natural as possible when trying to make a sale.

#3 Start slow and steady

As a salesperson, you may be a smooth talker. Talks and reasons may come to you effortlessly and you enjoy narrating them. However, selling is not all about ranting about what we know.

On meeting a prospective buyer, DO NOT even mention what you are selling during the first ten minutes. If you want to start talking about your product, prospective buyers will simply shut you out and no matter what you say, they are not going to buy anything.

Ideally, let your customers speak and listen carefully to know what they want. Your initial silence will go a long way in making the customer feel that you are really interested in helping them out if you can hear them out.

#4 Express instead of impress

Instead of impressing your customers be expressive and derive the same out of them. Do not use too much sales jargon such that they have to interpret your sales data. Rather, keep your selling approach simple and effortless. Shun the belief that buyers make their mind after watching glossy or flashy presentation. Rather, it makes them distracted from the real profile of the product.

#5 Create an irresistible offer

There are plenty of products or services out for sale on various platforms. To make your product outstanding, you have to offer what others haven't or cannot. If a product is sold for $200 and you are selling it for $200 only, no rampage would take place. Try selling the same product for just $199 and you will be amazed at how people can do everything to save even that $1.

#6 Take after-sale responsibility

Most of salespersons are usually just quick to sell you a product without even taking after-sales responsibility. This is a clear demarcation between a good and a bad salesperson. In order to carry on ethical selling, one simply cannot remain alienated from what happens to the product or service after the selling point.

Selling should include a satisfying experience that would come if the seller guides the buyers over after-sale problems. There needs to be effective interaction via feedback forms so that customers can give their feedback or ask for after-sales service.

#7 Guarantee quality or money back

One simple way to sell without losing your soul is to either deliver quality or return a customer's hard earned money. The money-back policy works like a charm, as the customer decides to try without any pitfalls for him. A smart seller would not just sell a product but also rather sell the end result that would endorse their product even further. Buyers will then get comfortable and fearless in buying.

#8 Sell without being devious

Selling without any devious methods helps in building long term bonds. Once buyers are convinced about getting quality products or services from you, they will definitely become loyal customers. Don't just concentrate on 'selling'. Make your selling a worthwhile opportunity that will empower the buyer with a quality product.

For example, you have with you a costly silk carpet with intricate embroidery. In a city, it would be priced for more than several thousand dollars. Now you took it to countryside and sold it for $200 worth of terracotta pots. The potter may feel happy to get such an exotic carpet. Actually, this deal is completely absurd and futile, since the carpet has no or little value to the potter and is likely to remain hidden in their storage area. As a salesperson, you do not qualify as making an ethical or sensible deal.

Let us rewind the situation and assume that you gave an automated potter's wheel worth $100 to that potter in exchange of his terracotta pots. Now, this would be a sensible deal for the potter, as that automated wheel will help him in making many more pots in the future. He would be able to obtain a lot more value from the product you sold him for many years to come.

Consider all possibilities

The very fact that you have a brilliant idea does in no way imply that you are 'sorted' when it comes to being on the path to entrepreneurial success. You have to understand that there will be a lot of hurdles along the way, which could indeed lead to a lot of disappointment should things go askew in the process of setting up that business.

Of course you need to be mentally prepared for the same; the last thing you want is to be discouraged by the potential hurdles that come along your path, to the point where you want to throw it all away.

By being apprised of the hurdles that might come along, you are preparing yourself to be a lot more resilient than you otherwise would have been, thus paving the way for you to face any obstacle that might come your way. In fact, some of the most successful entrepreneurs out there are those that have embraced failure time and again, simply because they believed to the core in the ideas that they felt would change the world.

Of course it is vital that you have a great business idea to begin with. Sometimes you might just get that 'Eureka!' moment when you're sitting in a mall and observing things around you. But in addition to the pointers that we have discussed, one also needs to do a thorough amount of research into the idea that they have stumbled upon, in order to assess its viability in the market out there.

Chapter 3 NLP (Neuro-Linguistic Programming)

We have delved into the art of persuasion, what it is, and how to start practicing your ability to persuading others. We have discussed how to understand others, and how understanding others can benefit you in your goals. We know that gaining and using influence to achieve our desires is possible. We have even discussed mind-control and many of its methods, and how to put these methods to everyday use. Now, we are digging deeper, into the world of Neuro-Linguistic Programming, or NLP for short.

NLP was founded and introduced by Richard Brandler and John Grinder in Santa Cruz, California in the 1970's amidst the Human Potential Movement. The Human Potential Movement was a psychotherapeutic movement that took a humanistic approach to people and their woes. The focus during this movement was personal psychological growth and understanding through many techniques. The most emphasized of these techniques were the use, application, and participation of encounter groups, sensitivity training, and primal therapy.

Encounter groups were a new way of thinking in the therapy world. Individuals participating in this type of therapy met as a group with a trainer to help guide their individual and collective process. Group sessions could last for hours, even days, and the length of the sessions was said to help members become uninhibited, literally exhausting its participants, allowing for an increase of self-awareness through verbal interactions that were not directed or influenced greatly by the trainer. Open displays of all range of emotions were welcomed and encouraged, even displays of rage, hostility, and grief.

Sensitivity training was encouraged to help people become more aware of their own prejudices, their own judgements and assumptions, and to become more sensitive and aware of others and their diversities within their group or workplace. Unstructured discussions amongst the group were encouraged to help increase empathy and embrace differences. This type of training is still popular and is often used within business and corporate models to increase harmony among employees and management.

Primal therapy was introduced by Dr. Arthur Janov. Dr. Janov believed that an individual's mental and physical ailments were a manifestation of repressed traumas, usually occurring in childhood. This type of treatment would begin with a patient seeing the therapist on-on-one for three weeks, concluding after fifteen sessions, to explore and get to the root of past traumas and how to overcome them. After the initial one-on-one sessions were completed, the individual patient was introduced to group therapy sessions once to twice a week, with no conclusion or time frame for completion. The focus on these group sessions was to allow patients a safe environment to lose control of their feelings and emotions to process their pain with assistance in a controlled environment, therefore alleviating the effect the trauma's they experienced and the effect those traumatic events had on their overall mental and physical health and well-being.

Now that you have a background on the Human Potential Movement of the 1970's, you will be able to better appreciate the theories behind the introduction of NLP into the world of psychotherapy. The ideas behind NLP are interesting to say the least, and it is important to note that many have discredited the applications and effectiveness of NLP because of what is claimed to be a lack of hard data to support the theories, and the belief that most of the theories of NLP are based on hypothesis only, that is, educated guesses or assumptions made by Bandler and Grinder during their research. Despite the naysayers, NLP is still used as a tool by many self-help personalities, corporations, educators, and psychotherapists today, as well as coaches and for business and management training groups.

The psychotherapeutic applications of NLP are to use the basic principles as a tool to successfully achieve success during instances of persuasion, in negotiations (either in business or personal matters), and during public speaking. For an individual to master the art of NLP, much practice and training will be required to achieve positive results, as NLP demands much control and subtlety. In fact, there are quite a few online workshops and certificate programs available, as well as physical schools dedicated to educating, instructing, and helping those interested in learning how to master the art of NLP. The theories behind NLP are very complex, and can be very hard for the layperson, or someone not familiar with the science and physiology behind the concepts of NLP to understand. In this book, we will introduce the principles and beliefs of what NLSP at is most basic concepts teaches, and how best a person being introduced to the concepts may begin to apply those concepts to achieve their desired goals.

Neuro-Linguistic Programming uses the premise that there is a connection between the language we speak, and the behavior patterns we all exhibit, and that both the way we speak, what words we use, and the way we normally behave can be altered or changed by other's who use NLP to achieve their own goals. That is, that a practitioner of NLP can change or alter another person's normal behaviors or thought patterns. Per the practitioners of NLP, our behavior is best understood based on our five senses, and that our perceptions of reality are subjective and different to everyone based on which of our senses is most prominent at the time of engagement, and that each person's ruling sensory interpretation changes regularly.

In easier terms, NLP states that linguistics (or language) is more than just words we speak, but also how our individual brains process and interpret these communications. Individual processing of this information is stressed, as another vital aspect of NLP is that no two people process and interpret information in the same way. Again, it is important to note that all five senses play a factor in our perception of our lives. So, in theory, by using the practices underlined in NLP, an individual's perception of their reality, their lives, can be altered for the better. Here it should be mentioned that not all people research and study NLP for the sole purpose of practicing NLP techniques on others, but also on themselves to better their life circumstances, or to change things they perceive to be negative in their lives.

To begin the practice of NLP on another person, the most valuable and important aspect is to begin to build a rapport with the other party, or to already have built rapport with the person in question. Rapport is a close relationship that includes mutual understanding of one another's feelings, and an ability to communicate well between yourself and the other party. Rapport is something that you have already built with a close friend or acquaintance, or a family member. When considering the requirements and steps that are needed to begin trying to practice the concepts of NLP on another person, other than already having a close relationship with said individual in question, your influence and the esteem or authority with which the other party views you are significant factors. It is much less difficult to build rapport with someone who looks up to you, sees you as a figure or authority, or defers to you and your knowledge.

So now that you have built rapport with another person, what's next?

The notion is to now begin layering very subtle meaning into your spoken or written interactions with the other person, to begin to implant suggestions in a very light and subconscious way. By stressing key words or phrases when communicating, you are highlighting these key words, and the other person's brain is subconsciously recognizing or remembering them without them being fully aware of what is occurring within their own body. Again, it is important to stress that subtlety is key. Another way to achieve the layered meanings you want to achieve is to use metaphors that can be interpreted in different ways, and the use of double-entendres. An example of a double-entendre was a very ironic and humorous quote by the late Hollywood actress Mae West. Mae once stated "Marriage is a fine institution, but I'm not ready for an institution.". What Mae was getting at is that while the institution of marriage is good and well for others that chose to get married, it also could make those that did marry crazy enough to be institutionalized. It is funny, a play on words, and has a clear double meaning and is open for interpretation.

Emotional speaking, or talking about things that will illicit an emotional response within the other person is also very useful. Knowing what words, phrases, stories, or double-entendres will illicit an emotional response will depend upon how well you know the individual or group of person's you are speaking to. If you understand the other's motivation or the reason being why they want to listen to you. Speak to what you think will create emotion within them. What emotion do you want them to feel? What words make you feel the way you want them to feel? What words make you feel happy? Joy, fun, pleasure, satisfaction, glee, bliss, ecstasy, all are words that convey and illicit happiness. A great example of stimulating a specific emotion, the emotions of optimism and change were invoked in millions of American's during Barack Obama's presidential campaign. The simple phrase, "Yes We Can", along with the simplistic imagery used causes a nationwide emotional response. Simple, to the point, and very effective. When speaking to other's emotions, simple and short is the most effective way to create a specific response in others. The shorter a message is, the more likely the other party's brain will retain it. Our brains can only contain so much information at a time, and it is best to not overload another person with long winded speeches or dialogues. Make an impact. Stress a sentence or phrase that you know will produce the emotional response you hope it does, and then emphasize it by using similar words throughout the communication.

Now that you have built rapport with someone, and you are actively using subtle layering techniques, and speaking to the person's emotions, it is time to become very observant. Watch the tiny non-verbal cues the other party exhibits during this interaction to modify the way you speak to them. Are they moving their eyes away from you, looking at you directly, rolling their eyes to the side? Is there any indication that you need to rephrase a sentence, or use alternative word choices based on how they react? Are their pupils dilating or constricting? Pupillary response is physiological and not a voluntary reaction that is controllable. Pupil dilation as it relates to emotional reaction may indicate sexual arousal, curiosity, or cognitive workload (as in, you are making them think). Pupil constriction can be a sign of a negative response, like fight-or-flight responses are being demonstrated in the body and it is time for you to re-direct the conversation, or disengage altogether and attempt your communication goals later. The faster a pupillary reaction occurs, the stronger their emotional response to the interaction is. Being able to notice pupillary response is something that is easy to practice on a day to day basis, but difficult to master.

Other non-verbal cues that need to be considered are flushing of the skin, their body language, and whether you feel they are being honest with their exchanges, or if there is any indication that they are falsifying certain details, giving false responses, or outright lying. Lying is hard work for the brain, so people who are not telling the truth must work harder at communicating as opposed to people that are being honest and open. People that are lying tend to leave small details out of their stories or responses, as it is easy to forget what specifics were given while lying. If someone mentions a concert they recently attended, but they leave out details or cannot recall what the opening set was, chances are, they aren't being honest. Memory, or the lack of one is another tale. Those that embellish or lie often claim to have a lacking memory, as it is harder to get caught up in a lie if you "can't remember" the information being asked. Correcting what is said is another easy way to tell if someone is not being honest, especially if the individual corrects themselves repeatedly during the interaction. Contradicting information or statements is also a dead giveaway, as is being fidgety, seeming to be nervous or preoccupied, or tense. Just like watching pupil reaction and other non-verbal cues, it is all about keen observation of the overall physical response the other person is exhibiting. Observing other people on this level in an imperceptible way takes a lot of time and practice to master, but with time, your brain can quickly take note of another person's emotional reactions and non-verbal tales. This is important, because it enables you to be able to change their response or way of thinking by interpreting what they are thinking, how you are making them feel, and deciding how to best change their response or thinking to match your own.

The next step in implementing NLP strategies after you have carefully and strategically observed the other person or people, is to then begin to mimic them. By imitating the other persons, you are attempting to create subconscious affiliation with them. This affiliation is another way for those individuals to feel a closer connection with you, as you are similar, even if it is a connection that is solely felt by your generation of it. Other important things to consider mirroring are their mannerisms, and their speech patterns. As mentioned previously, NLP is an art form that takes practice, less your efforts be noticed. If you are not subtle with your techniques, and another person realizes that you are taking on their own affects, they will immediately feel as though you are mocking or imitating them, and many see this as a negative and extremely offensive. Remember, the goal is to get them to trust you, to see you as an ally, someone they could easily have a meaningful connection with, not some hack that is fake or false in their interactions.

Once a rapport has been built, and you have observed non-verbal social queues, created an emotional and significant bond by your design through subtle simulation, it is time to put all your efforts to use. Allow and encourage the other person to talk about themselves, and continuing to be engaged. At the same time, you need to allow the other party to see a sense of openness and vulnerability within yourself, in a real and honest way. It has been stated before, and is now being reiterated again, that people sense falseness, and being fake in your interactions and willingness to be open to them in turn will be admonished. So, by engaging another party or group of people with this give and take will allow an opportunity, created by your own hard work and practices, for others to trust you and what you have to say. Gaining that trust is paramount, as it allows you to begin to steer the conversation in the direction you wish it to go. Steering other's thoughts in the direction you desire allows you the opportunity to set up the exchange to your benefit, and ultimately, gives you the upper hand in getting what you want, persuading others that your ideas or goals are the most logical and accurate, and that you want what everyone else wants too. Remember to elicit emotional states and responses in others as you continue to steer the scenario. Anchoring, again, slight nuanced touch to the upper arm in a natural and quick fashion only furthers your goal. And your goal is easier reached when following these practices that the NLP techniques offers you.

Chapter 4 NLP Techniques To Influence People

There are many different NLP techniques that can be used to improve your persuasive power, in many different situations. Each technique can be used by itself or in combination with other techniques to create fresh and effective methods of influence and "mind control". Let's see what you can deploy during your conversations, sales pitch or any other form of communication and speech.

Anchoring

Anchoring is a useful NLP technique for inducing a certain frame of mind or emotion, such as happiness or relaxation, very quickly and automatically. Usually, the "anchor" is a simple gesture, such as a touch or a word, that works as a bookmark for a desired feeling. By associating this particular gesture with the desired emotion, you can recall the latter whenever you want, just by using that same anchor.

How to use Anchoring

First, let's see how you can apply this techniques to your own life. Now, take the time to remember a situation when you were truly happy and excited, such as when you won a competition, had your first kiss, or had some really good news. It can be anything you like, as long as it was definitely an exciting time.

Describe to yourself the whole story of what happened leading up to that happy moment. Be vivid, and describe exactly how it felt, don't forget the details. Picture that moment in your head, and recall the feeling of happiness and excitement.

Now, gently and quickly squeeze your right thumb and index together, a couple times. As you do the second squeeze, make the picture of the happy moment larger, bringing it closer to you, and imagine the energy and excitement of that moment multiply in strength.

Describe again how you are feeling, especially what you were thinking at the time. As you do so, squeeze your fingers twice again. On that second finger squeeze, the happy feeling doubles, again. The more vibrant you can imagine that emotion, the better this technique will work. Repeat these steps until you have both described and doubled the passion of the feeling five times in a row.

Congratulations, you just laid the anchor. You just psychologically associated that little gesture with a powerful feeling. The next time you want to boost your energy and excitement, you can simply recall this anchor by using the exact same double-squeeze.

Do you remember the famous experiment by Russian scientist Ivan Pavlov? He rang a bell every time his dogs were fed. In a short time, the dogs started to associate the experience of eating with the sound of the bell. It didn't take much time till the dogs would start salivating at the mere ringing of the bell. This is similar to what you're doing when using the Anchoring technique.

How can you apply Anchoring?

You can use this powerful technique in seduction. When you get the girl to share a happy memory, an exciting moment or a previous sexual experience, and she's smiling, laughing or getting turned on, you can use either a distinct gesture or a light touch on the arm as an anchor. Whatever you choose, the anchor shouldn't be too noticeable, otherwise it will appear unusual and the effect will fail.

You can also anchor a specific feeling using music. Whenever I travel for business or to join masterminds and inner circles, I always listen to one song, or two different songs maximum. This way, I'm associating the feeling of self-worth and excitement for a new adventure with that particular song. When I'll be back home, I can recall those feelings just by listening to that song.

Now that you know how Anchoring works, you can apply it immediately next time you feel great, unstoppable and powerful. Whenever that happens, anchor that feeling with a simple gesture. It may be something involving the fingers as we saw earlier, or maybe punching your chest like a gorilla, or maybe barking a couple times and clapping your hands. Just remember to "save" every powerful emotion you experience, because you can use it weeks or months later when you need an energy boost.

Pattern Interruption

This is an effective technique for installing keywords into your listener's subconscious mind. You can also combine it with other NLP techniques, such as anchoring, to give him a message that, for reasons unknown to him, appears very profound or significant.

Pattern interruption works by luring the listener's inner monologue or even their pure unconscious train of thought into a pattern or sequence. When that pattern is established, you then jolt them out of that pattern at a critical moment before the pattern completes. This leaves the listener's unconscious mind waiting for the next part of the pattern to occur, while their conscious mind is distracted.

So what exactly is Pattern Interruption?

Let's use an analogy. Say you had an old man who has a pet dog to do all his actions for him. The old man represents our conscious mind and the dog represents the unconscious mind. The man (conscious) makes the decisions, and the dog (unconscious) performs various necessary actions for that man.

Step one. We ask the old man for a sandwich. The man then asks his dog to go get some bread, slice some cheese, put it on a plate, and bring to me.

Follow me so far?

Step two. We ask the old man for another sandwich. The man then gives his dog the same sequence of commands. The dog gets the bread, slices the cheese, puts it on the plate, and SLAP! We slap the man in the face and ask him to do a dance. Before the dog has been given the final command for the sandwich (bring to me) the pattern has been interrupted and new commands given.

The old man (conscious mind) being far less clever than to dog (unconscious mind) has forgotten all about that final stage of the sandwich pending. But the dog has not forgotten. The dog cannot speak to the man, but is thinking "what about the command 'bring it to me' which I still haven't done yet?" The dog will keep thinking of this last command for quite a while.

Step three. If I'm mean, I can ask the old man to give me his wallet. The man might ask his dog "hey dog, I'm thinking about giving you a command to bring my wallet to me. I'm not sure, is "bring it to me" something you would normally do?"

The dog might say "well yes, I've been waiting to a command like that." And the dog will bring me the wallet.

Swish

The Swish technique, also known as Swish Pattern, is very helpful if you want to replace an unfavourable emotion or behaviour with a more beneficial one. You can use this technique to improve your life in a lot of different ways, such as making going to the gym more fun or making healthy foods taste better.

You know your computer's "copy and paste" function, right? Well, the Swish technique is pretty similar. On your computer, you copy some text and then you paste it somewhere else. Using this neuro-linguistic trick, you can take part of a memory or neurological tag and paste it over the tag of a different memory.

To fully comprehend the NLP Swish, you should know that every memory has emotions attached to it. Good memories have some good emotions attached to them, while the contrary is true for bad memories. Let's see how the NLP Swish can be used to "edit" your emotional tags.

Let's imagine that you're a teenager who just moved to a new town, and tomorrow is your first day at your new school. Of course, you don't know anyone there. This situation may make you feel anxious, worried or nervous. Yet you know that by feeling this way, you'll be in your head and come across weird to others, thus making it more likely that you'll be alienated. It's like a downward spiral.

So what's happening here? You're basically associating the feeling of anxiety with the condition of the first day at a new school. Now, it's time to use the Swish technique to associate a feeling of excitement instead.

First of all, you pick a good memory that is associated with excitement - such as anticipation of going to a girl's house for the first time, a party with friends or an amazing trip. Focus deeply on how you feel, concentrate on the adrenaline rush and excitement that grow inside your body at the prospect of a great adventure - now picture that situation in your mind and SWISH!, quickly swap it with the picture of going to school tomorrow. Next, before any feeling of anxiety starts to rise, swish again! - swap the picture back to the good memory.

The whole process is very simple: you have to keep focusing on how excited you felt, and hold onto that feeling. While maintaining the positive emotion in your mind, swish back and forth quickly between the two pictures. Soon, you'll be able to associate that positive feeling to the new condition, which was causing you anxiety.

Loop Break

Loop Break is an experimental NLP technique that allows you to consciously change or stop an unconscious process. Your body uses naturally particular looping processes to enter various states such as fear, rage, anger, anxiety and stress: this technique works by breaking those patterns.

You can use the NLP loop break to control your own behavior, and by mastering this technique you'll be able to induce a loop break in someone else to help them control their own behavior. It's a very simple NLP technique but simplicity is often the best option.

When someone is about to experience anger, they usually need a trigger. Imagine this scenario: you're driving to an important meeting and you're already late. The journey is long and you're already feeling quite stressed. Then, at the traffic lights, someone rear-ends your car. This is the trigger that will make your stress explode into anger.

It might feel good to get out and yell at the guy behind you, but it may escalate things, and it certainly isn't productive. The most efficient action is to quickly get his license plate and insurance details, then be on your way back to the meeting. However, because of all the anger and stress that are boiling inside you, your cognitive ability is weakened, and you can even end up in a pointless argument or fight.

Now, let's see exactly what is happening in our brains during highly emotional states like this. The reason our emotions add up so quickly is that there's a loop occurring between our memory, our amygdala (the region of the brain responsible for emotion), and our body, which is bypassing our frontal lobes, the region of the brain responsible for moderating our behavior.

In a situation of stress, the hypothalamus orders the body to get ready by increasing the heart rate and tending muscles. The body obeys, now there's tension in the muscles rising up and the heart starts to beat faster. Now it's the turn of the memory, which recognizes this feeling and starts showing you some other memories that also include this feeling of stress. Lastly, the amygdala makes you feel the same exact feeling of stress associated with the past memories.

How can you break the loop with NLP?

Have you ever heard the suggestion "count to ten before you reply in anger"? Well, this is a form of NLP Loop Break at work. Basically, you just need to start up your frontal cortex to moderate your behavior. You can do this by consciously forcing a different emotion or bodily response. In the situation of stress above, this can be done just by counting to ten, or even better, having a pre-prepared "comfort thought" to remind yourself it's not really a big deal. As a comfort thought, you may have an exciting weekend trip coming up, or you might have a lovely wife or pet dog or anything that is a comfort for you. Once you have it in your mind, you'll be able to start laughing at the stressful situation, even jeering it for not being able to spoil your life.

This is what a successful loop break looks like.

Your body raised your heart rate and built tension in your muscles. Your memory matches the current feeling with stress, thus showing you other memories associated with that feeling.

Now the conscious mind starts playing its role: you decide you don't want to be stressed. You're going to loop break this process! You can count up to ten or use your comfort thought. You're comforted by the thought that this stressful situation, no matter how unpleasant, does not have the power to take away the amazing holiday you've planned for the next weekend.

The amygdala now makes you feel anticipation and excitement. The conscious mind can now laugh at the stressful situation, because it doesn't have power over your emotions anymore.

Framing

The framing technique is a sort of emotional amplifier or de-amplifier, which works by correcting links in your limbic system between your amygdala and your hippocampus. That's a thousand dollars phrase to say that this technique can help you see things differently, i.e. framing them in a different way compared to what you're used to.

What makes this technique so effective is its simplicity; it can also be easily applied in conjunction with other NLP techniques. First, let's see why this is so important. It's known that we learn lessons in life from both bad and good memories. We perceive them as bad or good, but in reality memories are emotionless highlight reels of past situations and events.

In fact, memories and emotions are stored and produced by different parts of the brain. Given that those two parts of the brain are right next to each other, but they are still separate parts of the brain. The hippocampus stores and produces your memories, and the amygdala is responsible for your emotions.

Since the emotions are separate from the memories, it must be possible to change the emotions associated with a particular memory. That's when the Framing technique comes into play, by editing your emotional response to a specific memory. How does it work?

Step one: take a memory that you've associated bad feelings with. It can be anything negative, like a job interview gone wrong or the last argument you had with your mother. Now reduce the highlight reel to a single snapshot that represents that memory.

Now go ahead and step back from this memory. Don't look at the situation with your own eyes, but look at it from above. If you already used a 3rd person perspective, take a further step back so you are slightly further away than before.

So now you can see yourself, in a single snapshot that represents the bad event. Now make the picture black and white. Make it a little bit blurry or out of focus, like a very old photo.

It's now time to put the picture into a frame: you can choose any frame you want, from an old fashioned heavy frame to a modern stainless steel one. Take it and put it on the wall, in an art gallery, or in a restaurant, wherever you want. Try different lighting on the painting. Watch other people look at the painting, then move on.

How does the bad situation feel now? Is it still as stressful? Try again, repeat this process and it should further reduce the bad influence on your emotions.

Your mind is treating the memory more like just a picture. It helps detach you emotionally from a memory, so that you can have a clear and unaffected view on it, without letting bad emotions overwhelm you.

You can also apply this technique the other way around, so instead of weakening the bad emotional response to a memory, you can also take a normal memory and amplify the emotional response into strong, vivid feelings.

Meta Model

The NLP Meta Model is a therapeutic technique that can help you understand other people's problems or help them understand their own problems better. This means to deconstruct what someone is saying so you can find the underlying cause of the problem.

Often, when someone has a problem, they unconsciously already know the solution inside their mind. Most people do not like the obvious solution, so they keep stirring the problem in hopes that a new, easier solution will come up. The Meta Model technique is designed to deconstruct the way someone words their problem, to get to the bottom of it. Let's analyze the following example of a conversation between you and your good friend Zack.

Zack: my wife can be so annoying sometimes!

You: Why, what's she doing?

This is the most common response in this situation. The problem is that it assumes the wife is actually doing something specific to annoy your friend Zack. To apply the Meta Model technique, your response should make as few assumptions as possible, like this:

Meta Response: What exactly is happening when you find yourself feeling the most annoyed?

We must make as few assumptions as possible because communication is not a clear-cut procedure. When you communicate, your message stems from various prompts such as memories and emotions, and sent through a web of cognitive processes before it leaves your mouth. Therefore, it stands to reason that it is not easy to 100% effectively communicate the exact message you want to convey.

Chapter 5 Halo Effect

Did you know attractive students get better grades?

Did you know attractive criminals get shorter sentences and are more likely to get parole?

Did you know taller CEOs and CEOs with deeper voices get paid more?

This somewhat unfair phenomenon is known as the halo effect. The halo effect refers to the fact that us humans have a tendency to judge a person based on one attribute. For example:

- Attractive students. People have a tendency to assume that attractive people are smarter. Research shows that teachers give attractive students better grades—even though their very attractiveness makes them more likely to spend less time studying and instead party more, have more sex, use illicit drugs, etc.

- Unattractive students. People have a tendency to assume that ugly people are less intelligent. Research shows that teachers tend to give unattractive students worse grades.

- Criminals. People also have a tendency to assume that attractive people are more morally upright while ugly people are less so. Studies have found that ugly people get harsher sentences and are less likely to get parole while the opposite is true for attractive people.

- Job applicants. Employers rate applicants that are attractive or likable as more intelligent, competent, and qualified.

While the four above examples touched on how the halo effect can apply to one's attractiveness, the halo effect also applies to many other areas.

For example: wealth, confidence, competence in a specific domain, likeability, etc.

Because of the halo effect, people often assume that wealthy people have good qualities in all areas of life. That they must be good at everything, while poor people must be lazy slobs who are "no good for nuthin."

Similarly, because of the halo effect, people intuitively equate confidence with competence (even though the shy engineer is probably more competent than the ultra-confident salesman.

Because of the halo effect, people also assume that people that are skilled in one area must be good at everything else, too. For example, the sports superstar must also be a great businessman, great father, good in bed, a great writer, an above average driver, and so on.

The halo effect can also apply to products. Many brands create a top of the line product so that people will perceive their more affordable offerings to be better as well.

Now, what does any of this have to do with you? How can the halo effect help you to influence and persuade?

Here's how: exploit the halo effect to make people perceive you to be more intelligent, competent, and just overall better in all areas of life. Do this, and you'll have a much, much easier time influencing people.

That begs the question: what can you do to give yourself a "halo" that causes people to perceive you more positively in every way? Read on to find out...

How To Use The Halo Effect To Your Advantage

To help uncover some of the factors you can use to benefit from the halo effect, let's take a look at one of the first studies conducted on the halo effect: "A Constant Error in Psychological Ratings" by Edward Thorndike.

Thorndike got two commanding officers to fill out a survey evaluating their soldiers in terms of the following qualities:

- Physical qualities. Neatness, voice, physique, posture, and energy.

- Personal qualities. Intelligence, leadership skills, loyalty, dependability, selflessness, cooperation, and responsibility.

The purpose of Thorndike's study was to find out how the ratings of one characteristic affected the ratings of other characteristics.

The results? Thorndike reported that, "The correlations are too high and too even." Soldiers that had their physiques rated high also got high ratings for intelligence, leadership, and character.

Likewise, Thorndike discovered that soldiers who had one of their attributes rated negatively had all of their other attributes rated negatively, too.

So while you can benefit from the halo effect, you can also—if you're not careful—give yourself a disadvantage with the so-called "horns effect" (which refers to the devil's horns).

So, for example, you might be by far the most skilled person in your company, but if you're fat, dress like a slob, and lack confidence, charisma, and clarity of expression, people are going to perceive you negatively and assume you're not much good at anything.

So then, how can you make sure to benefit from the halo effect?

Here are a few different ways you can get the halo effect to work in your favor:

- Dress well. Be clean, well-groomed, and wear flattering clothes that fit (very) well and/or are tailored.

- Be likable. You don't need to be an eager-to-please pushover who doesn't know how to say "no," but it is important to be friendly, get along with people, and overall be a likable person.

- Be confident. People who are confident are perceived by others to be more competent, intelligent, qualified, etc.

Chapter 6 Traps of persuasion

Persuasiveness is an effective aptitude everybody ought to learn. It is helpful in incalculable circumstances. For both your business and your personal life, being inspiring and influential to others will be the foundation for accomplishing objectives and being successful.

Learning about the traps of persuasion will give you new awareness for when they appear in sales messaging you read. The greatest advantage? Your cash stays in your pocket. It literally pays for you to understand exactly how sales representatives and marketers offer you items that you don't really require. The following are some persuasive techniques that work on a subconscious level.

Outlining Impacts Thought

Let's say you're thirsty, and someone hands you a glass of water not-quite full. "The glass is half full." An optimist would "outline" the reality of your glass of water in that way. Outlining is used as an approach to modify how we classify, connect, and attach meaning to every aspect of our lives.

The headline "FBI Operators Surround Cult Leader's Compound" creates a mental picture strikingly different from another version of the headline for the same story: "FBI Specialists Raid Small Christian Gathering of Women and

Children." Both headlines may convey what happened, however, the selected words affect the readers' mental and emotional responses, and therefore direct the impact the target events have on the article's readers.

Outlining is employed by apt government representatives. For example, representatives on both sides of the abortion debate refer to their positions as "pro-choice" or "pro-life." This is intentional, as "pro" has a more positive association to build arguments on. Outlining an event, product, or service this way unobtrusively utilizes emotional words strategically to persuade individuals to see or accept your perspective.

Creating a convincing message is as easy as selecting words that summon strategic pictures in the minds of your audience. Indeed, even with neutral words surrounding it, a solitary stimulating word can be powerful.

Reflecting as Persuasive Strategy

Reflecting, often called "the chameleon effect," is the act of replicating the movements and non-verbal communication of the individual you want to persuade. By mirroring the actions of the individual listening, you create an appearance of empathy.

Hand and arm motions, inclining forward or reclining away, or different head and shoulder movements are types of non-verbal communication you can reflect. We, as a whole, do this without much thought, and now that you're becoming aware of that, you'll notice not only yourself but others doing it, as well.

It is important to be graceful, thoughtful about it and allow just a couple seconds to pass between their movements and you reflecting them.

Highlight Scarcity of a Product or Service

The concept of scarcity is often employed by marketers to make products, services, or associated events and deals appear to be all the more engaging on the grounds that there will be restricted accessibility. The belief is that there is a huge amount of interest for it if availability is scarce. For example, an ad for a new product might say: Get one now! They're selling out quickly!

Again, it literally pays to know that this is a persuasion strategy that you will see everywhere. Consider this concept the next time you settle on your buying choice. This principle triggers a feeling of urgency in most individuals, so it is best used when applied in your marketing and sales copy.

Reciprocity Helps Make a Future Commitment

When somebody helps us out, we feel responsible to provide a proportional payback. All in all, the next time you need someone to accomplish something beneficial for you, consider doing something unexpectedly pleasant for them first.

At work, you could pass a colleague a lead. At home, you could offer to loan some landscaping tools to a neighbor.

The details, where or when you do it, won't make a difference; the key is to supplement the relationship without being sought out first. Lead with value and give it freely, without overtly expecting anything in return, and their response will come.

Timing Can Bolster Your Good Fortune

Individuals will be more pleasant and accommodating when they're mentally exhausted. Before you approach somebody for something they may not otherwise participate in, consider holding back until they've recently accomplished something mentally challenging. Consider making your offer toward the end of the work day, for example, when you can get a colleague or collaborator on the way out of the office. Whatever you may ask, a reasonable reaction could be, "I'll deal with it tomorrow."

Enhance Compliance to Acquire a Needed Result

To avoid cognitive dissonance, we all try to be true to how we've acted in the past. A reliable technique business people use is to shake your hand as they are consulting with you. We have been taught that a handshake equals a "sealed deal," and by doing this before the arrangement is really sealed, the business person has taken a step to persuade you into believing the deal is already done.

One approach to employing this yourself is influencing individuals to act before their minds are made up. Let's say that you are roaming downtown with a companion, and you decide you want to go see a movie at the local theater; yet, your companion is undecided. Compliance can come into play if you begin strolling toward the theater while they are still thinking about it. Your companion will probably consent to go once they realize you are strolling in the theater's direction.

Attempt Fluid Discourse

In the natural flow of our speech, interjections and reluctant expressions act as fillers when we need a moment to think or select the "right" word, for example, "um" or "I mean," and obviously the newly pervasive "like." These fillers have the unintended impact of making us appear to be unsure and doubtful and, in this way, less convincing. When you're certain about your message, others will be more effectively persuaded.

If you have trouble finding the right words at the right time, practice some free-flow association every day in front of the mirror for 60 seconds. You can add it to your morning ritual, or you can do it while having a shower, like I usually do. Basically, your goal in these 60 seconds is to jump from one topic to another very quickly, by associating words; do your best to avoid "um," "like," or other fillers.

Example: The water on my back right now is so hot, it reminds me of the hot weather in California. I love Cali; I like the food there. Mexican food is so spicy and hot, like Mexican women. I remember Marcella, that one Mexican girl I met last time I was there; she was probably the only blonde girl from Mexico. She was blonde like a Swedish model. I've never been to Sweden, but I've heard it's cold out there...

And so on, until you get to 60 seconds without pauses or interjections. Once you reach that point after some practice, you can aim for 120 seconds. Once you've done that, the next step is to practice this game with other people. You don't need to go on for a full two minutes straight, but while you're talking to someone, you can go on a tangent for 20 seconds and practice the free-flow association skill. You'll practice and improve tremendously, while they'll be wondering "This guy is interesting. I really want to know what he's going to say next..."

Group Affinity Can Affect Decisions

We have a much higher tendency to imitate or be persuaded by somebody we like or by somebody we see as an influential leader.

A compelling approach to make this work for you, bolstering your good fortune, is to be viewed as a leader by your target audience—regardless of whether you officially have the title. It helps to be enchanting and sure, so individuals will have more confidence in your message. Keep improving yourself, and you'll soon become more magnetic than everyone else.

If you're interacting with an individual who doesn't consider you to be a powerful person (for example, a rival at work or your irritating in-laws), you can, in any case, exploit group affinity. For example, if you praise a leader that individual respects, that praise then activates the positive associations in that individual's brain about that admired leader, which creates a mental space where they can relate those qualities with you.

Create a Photo Opportunity with Man's Best Friend

Give your target audience the idea that you're trustworthy, and motivate them to be loyal to you, by taking a photo of yourself with a pooch (it doesn't need to be your own puppy). This can make you appear kind and cooperative, but keep these kinds of photo-ops to a minimum; setting up an excessive number of pictures looks amateurish. On a side note, it pays to know your audience; if you know they share a lot of cat pictures, maybe try a picture or two with a feline friend, too.

Offer a Drink

This might seem too easy, but giving the individual you want to persuade a warm drink to hold while you're conversing with them can be persuasive in itself. The warm vibe you've offered their hands (and their body) can intuitively make them see you as candidly warm, affable, and inviting. Offering a chilly drink can do the opposite! As a rule, individuals tend to feel "frosty" and seek out warm beverages when they're feeling stressed or overwhelmed, so take care of that need keeping in mind the end goal to make them more open.

Start with a Simple "Yes" Question

Start the discussion with an inquiry that creates a "Yes" reaction. "Nice weather we're having, isn't it?" or "You're searching for a great price on a car, right?"

When you get somebody saying yes, it's anything but difficult to motivate them to proceed, up to and including "Yes, I'll get it." You can counter this in your daily life by giving cautious answers to even the simplest questions.

Gently Break the Contact Boundary

You could be sealing a deal or asking somebody out for coffee, and touching them (in a modest and suitable way) can enhance your odds of hearing "Yes," because you have intuitively triggered the human yearning to connect.

In a professional setting, it is normally best to "touch" verbally by giving consolation or acclaim, as a physical touch could be seen as lewd behavior.

In sentimental circumstances, any delicate touch from a lady will more often than not be taken well. Men will need to proceed here with extreme caution—keeping in mind the end goal is to abstain from making a lady feel uncomfortable.

Chapter 7 Suggestion And Persuasion Techniques

As a spy, I had to face some high-pressure situations where communication above all else was my biggest weapon. Some of these situations arose during my interviews and training and but many while out on the job. However it was always critical to keep a calm composure and make the most of the situation even when things looked dire.

One of the worst things you can do in a high pressure situation is to show the other party that you are uncomfortable. In my line of work, losing your composure is one of the quickest ways to blow your cover. In casual or business interactions, losing your composure can show everything from nervousness, fear, and a general lack of confidence.

The key to keeping your composure is in suppressing the 'fight or flight' response I have mentioned previously. Anxiety can also cause this. From the second adrenaline starts pumping through your system, your ability to perceive the situation shrinks. You will lose focus and be unable to think clearly. It can also cause a rapid heartbeat, sweating, and an array of other unwanted symptoms. You should avoid this at all costs.

The following is a guide on how you can control a situation such as this and the qualities you need to possess in order to tackle these instances effectively.

Communication

Communication is obviously the central theme to persuasion in general and in turn this book, but it is especially important when it comes to controlling a high-pressure situation. You have to start to think of things in a very elementary way. You will have to be in a position to explain something to someone in such a way that they will be able to explain it back to you without difficulty. That is how strong and clear your communication skills should be here. You must make use of clear language that uses only simple words and phrases for clarity that are not ambiguous or confusing in anyway. Think of everybody in the room as having only a beginner's grasp on the language you are speaking. This will force you to break it down to the clearest and most concise steps. Often times this would be me, speaking Russian in a room of Mafia members or Portuguese with government officials in Lisbon. Do not use overly complicated phrases which could be misinterpreted or misunderstood.

I often tell the story about my dealings with a section of the Russian mafia who were based out of Hungary at the time, in the capital Budapest to be precise. The story is actually more concerned with the exit strategy I had to employ to escape without getting killed. To quickly re-cap, I was held up in a tight spot trying to arrange a price for some unregistered guns I was trying to sell to this outfit. Things went bad pretty quickly and I ended up using a pre-planned escape route where an extraction team was waiting to fetch me out.

What I don't usually tell people is how the situation deteriorated to that point as in reality it is quite embarrassing for me to admit in truth. Russians can be difficult to deal with at the best of times and especially when they are suspicious or in a highly charged and vodka induced emotional state (which this crew definitely was at the time). It basically came down to communication or a lack of sufficient clarity on my part. My Russian was reasonably strong at this point, not as fluent as my Portuguese after spending considerable time in Brazil in the late 1990's before being the Lisbon station chief in the early 2000's.

But it was good enough to get by. However I had picked up somewhat of an unwanted habit after dating a local girl whilst based in St. Petersburg just a few years prior. Russians have a tendency to add diminutive suffixes to words that we can't really do in English. They often put these before nouns to make them softer sounding, for example "chik" will turn any masculine noun into something way less serious. There are lots of these suffixes and my girlfriend would use them all of the time. Now this is where it went bad for me, as I decided it would be a good idea to start using this type of language with the mafia guys in an attempt to soften the situation. I actually think I started to use the feminine "chka" by mistake. Needless to say it didn't work and these chaps took it as more of an insult to their masculinity more than anything. So that game and experiment was over for me that day but not without learning a serious lesson, always stick to the most basic, clear and least misinterpret able words possible in high stakes situations..."

Preparation

I'm big on preparation as you have probably already realized and the high stakes persuasion game is no different. One of the best ways to tackle a high-pressure situation is to be 100% be prepared for it. By remaining prepared for a situation, you will know what to say and do and what phrases to fall back on. Also you will be acutely aware of what your intensions and purpose were in the first place to remain focused and on track.

I have stated this before, but as a spy, most of the work that I did was based on psychological warfare. For interrogation, information extraction, or other reasons, learning about the individual and subsequently using psychological techniques to get what was needed was paramount. You had to research your mark and learn all you could, finding out how they will respond to various personality traits & behavioral patterns. Then adapt your own behavior accordingly to optimally get the most out of them.

So in order to effectively persuade someone especially in high stakes settings, you will have to anticipate the situation and know exactly how someone is likely to react ahead of time.

Combing this type of preparation with quick thinking and advanced persuasion skills is the recipe for winning here.

Adaptable Behavior

Remember that your behavior matters most in a situation like this. You will find that individual situations, as in life, especially these high stakes settings are never completely cut and dry. Regardless of your preparation, things will never go entirely how you anticipated, and that's OK. Remember that our body language counts for a lot and drives across the message to the other person for whatever emotions you are portraying. You need not necessarily to be in a powerful position in order to control a high-pressure situation as it is flexibility that matters more. You have to be able to adapt and do more behavior-wise in order to persuade someone.

Your personality should also be flexible enough to react and be able to call on the intuitive and relational persuasion skills you have built up. If you notice, children can be very persuasive as they have an array of habits to fall back on while trying to convince someone of something. Say a child wants a piece of candy; he will pout, cry, throw a tantrum, plead and even plant a kiss in order to get it. The parent, however, will have just one response to give which is saying "no" to the child. Similarly, you will only be able to control a situation if you showcase an array of behaviors that will garner the right response from your opponent and ultimately have command over the situation through your behavioral flexibility. Try to cultivate this into your thinking and practice adaptability wherever you can. Try to incorporate this into your day-to-day, when the stakes aren't high.

Emotions

Remember to leash your emotions as best you can during high-pressure situations. I talk a lot about how emotions can't be avoided during my discussion of negotiation principles, but that is more about inducing empathy in the everyday interactions we have. When it comes to highly charged high pressure situations it's a different story.

When these situations come about, most people will turn into becoming vulnerable. They will not be able to control their emotions and cause the situation to get out of hand. In such a case, it will be important to stay calm and not give away a negative reaction. This is, of course, easier said than done and will be important to remain patient. You will have to read a situation correctly and ensure that you know how to control your emotions. Remain as detached from it as possible so that your emotions lie well within your control.

Strong Belief

If you are sure about yourself and remain confident then you are much more likely to control a situation and persuade your opponent more effectively.

You have to be able to exude confidence so that the other person knows you are certain, people can relate to assertiveness and assurance in someone's mannerisms very easily and it will put everybody at ease especially in high stakes settings. With time and practice, you will be able to identify when these intense situations are likely to come about. You will be in a more comfortable position to persuade people when they do.

Chapter 8 Types Of Suggestions

If you are reading this, it's likely you are involved in persuading people to do things – buy something, request information, sign up for a subscription, "like" your Facebook page, and so on.

In fact, all of our lives are filled with persuasion tasks. Beyond persuading customers to do our will, we are constantly trying to elicit cooperation from family members, co-workers, and even strangers.

Sad Truth: We Are Lousy at Persuasion

In business, we are usually terrible persuaders. 98 out of 100 sales emails get no response. Similarly, 98 out of 100 direct mail pieces don't work. Even costly in-person sales calls fail more than nine times out of ten. And, on our websites, we often see many more visitors hitting the "back" button than doing what we'd like them to do.

Why are we so bad at persuasion? For one thing, it's difficult – just about all people have inertia that makes them reluctant to take any kind of action. Hitting the back button is easier than filling out your subscription form. Moving on is easier than getting out a credit card and completing the order process.

Often, the reason for inaction is simply that making no decision is usually easier than choosing to do something.

"Don't Confuse Me With Facts"

Another reason for our failure to persuade is that we ignore both the science of persuasion and well-established business success factors.

Instead of using a structured, scientific approach to creating our website, print advertising, and other marketing content, we have meetings.

At these meetings, creative types throw out ideas they think will attract the customer's attention. Product managers tout features and benefits. Sales managers complain about the superior marketing efforts of competitors.

Eventually, ideas are filtered, compromises are made, and an ad campaign or website goes into production. Sometimes, this actually works. All too often, though, the results don't meet expectations.

There has to be a better way.

What we hope to accomplish here is to add structure to the persuasion process. We need a way to incorporate the logical arguments, the creative ideas, as well as proven techniques developed over decades of research in social science and other fields.

The framework in this book forces, or at least encourages, the people who use it to create advertisements, websites, and other kinds of persuasive content to consider both conscious and non-conscious elements.

This structured approach won't turn a 2% success rate into 100%. But, by ensuring we are appealing to the customer's conscious and non-conscious decision-making processes, we can hope to do a better job. When success rates are this low, even a modest improvement can have a big impact.

Science to the Rescue?

There's some good news, though. Scientists have been studying persuasion and decision-making for decades, and actually understand quite a bit about how the process works.

Robert Cialdini, the best-known scientist in the persuasion space, enumerated his now famous six key principles of influence decades ago.

Stanford's BJ Fogg developed the Fogg Behavior Model as well as the Behavior Wizard, both methods of describing the types of human behavior and how they can be changed.

We get other insights into behavior from a totally different field: evolutionary psychology. Scientists like Geoffey Miller show us that many of the behaviors of modern humans are rooted in our hunter-gatherer ancestry and talk about "mating cues." So, even though male viewers have about as much chance of "mating" with the sultry model in the fragrance ad as shaking the hand of the man in the moon, her sexy image may still prime them to buy the product.

While Nobel laureate Daniel Kahneman doesn't work directly in the persuasion space, his model for human decision-making is highly relevant. His research showed that we have two kinds of thought processes. System 1 is intuitive, emotional, and fast, while System 2 is conscious, logical, and relies more on reasoning.

In addition, we have researchers like Dan Ariely, Adam Alter, and many others who are constantly exposing specific (and often surprising) aspects of human behavior via their research.

Chapter 9 Why You Need Both Persuasion And Influence To Succeed

Now that we have discussed the importance of both persuasion and influence and how they differ, let's get into why you need both of them to succeed. Perhaps you have already found that you are good at one, but now it is time to develop the other so that you can live to your maximum potential. If you don't build your skills in both areas, it will show in other instances not always related to persuasion and influence. The best way to make sure that you are being as influential as possible is to use persuasion, and vice versa. It might not always feel as though you need both, but you will realize how important they work together to truly get what you want.

You do not have to have power over others to survive. Some people can successfully get their needs fulfilled on their own without any help from other people. However, if you do know how to get what you want from others, that technique can really expand your life into areas that you never could have imagined. If you want to live a happy life and get what you want, then you will need to be a persuasive influencer—it is the best way to encourage others to give you the things that you most desire.

Those who are influencers are not always the type of people who should be persuading others. There are some people who are natural influencers, but that skill isn't always for the best. These people might know how to scare people into believing what they have to say, or perhaps they use other methods of fear to try and get their points across. The best way to ensure that you are spreading positivity is to use your powers for good and stop those who are misguided from spreading their bad influence onto susceptible individuals. Our job as persuaders is to make sure that people aren't manipulated but are persuaded to do better instead.

Persuasion and influence paired together will give you the necessary confidence to elicit change. If you have what it takes to recognize positivity and encourage other people, you can really change the world on different levels.

Not everyone is going to find that power, but those who do encourage global change were also influenced by someone. Though you might feel helpless sometimes, remember that influencing one person can mean influencing another, and so on and so forth. Before you know it, your words could travel across the world to someone else. All it takes to see real positive change is the altering of one person's mind.

Though you might not be the one to inspire thousands of people, you might inspire twenty, and they each could go on to inspire twenty more, and then twenty more, and before you know it, many are forever changed by the ideas that you thought of in the first place.

You Can't Have One Without The Other

There is a difference between people who are inspiring and people who are influential, and you are reading this book because you want to learn how to influence. You may not be able to walk away from this book being persuasive, but by now you are more aware of those powers, so you can look for them in instances that you might have otherwise ignored. Recognizing these instances will help improve your own methods while also strengthening your ability to protect yourself from other people's negative persuasive techniques. When we are influential ourselves, it becomes much more difficult for people to take advantage of us.

Part of being an influencer is using small methods of persuasion. It starts by convincing one person to believe in you. From there, more people will follow, and before you know it, you have become an influencer who a lot of people admire. You might be the person they come to for advice, or perhaps you are the friend who everyone wants to have in their life. Either way, it all started with one small instance of persuasion that grew into something bigger.

If you continually try to persuade others but do not have an influential life, people are not going to be as attentive. If you consistently tell people what to do, but your own life is a mess, people most likely won't listen to anything you have to say. To be a better persuader, you have to put yourself in a position that other people desire. This theory is used in the basic method of advertising referenced earlier. When you want to sell a product, place it with someone attractive. People may buy that product with the hope of becoming attractive too. If you live an influential life and show other people that you know what it takes to be happy, they are more likely to listen to your persuasions.

Once you find the balance of both, they will become natural to you. An influencer usually knows how to be persuasive without even trying, simply because they have gotten to a point in their life where they know what is best.

Persuasion Comes Before Influencing

As you become more persuasive, you will become better at being influential. Some people are born into influential roles. Look at Kylie Jenner, for example, or other people who were seemingly born into a role of persuasion. They didn't do much other than be children of the wealthy or well known. People started to admire them, perhaps because they wanted to be like them, so these people ultimately became influencers.

Most of us aren't born into insanely wealthy families, so we do not have the luxury of being a natural influencer. For everyone else, it will start with smaller instances of persuasion. You will not only have to let others know that you believe you know best, but you must show that you actually do. You persuade people in small ways, maybe at work by giving advice where it is needed. Eventually, you become the person they go to for final decisions and other monumental moments that might have otherwise passed you by had you not been initially persuasive.

An influencer becomes who they are because they are able to persuade others. They have the ability to make people see their perspective, or just a different perspective. When someone is able to change one's perspective, they stand out from the crowd. As stated previously, a person is an influencer because they go against the current trend and aren't afraid to stand out. When a person is authentic, it can take them a long way in terms of the perception of other people. Some people are lost in their lives and need to look to other individuals for inspiration. If you are an influencer, you step into that role and become someone who inspires individuals to make different decisions.

If you can't be persuasive, you won't be influential. You might be admirable or inspirational, but you will not actually encourage anyone else to change. People may still like some of your qualities, but they won't really listen to you when it matters. Those who don't believe in what they have to say will be individuals who don't excel in persuasion. In order to make sure that you have what it takes to influence other people, you have to make sure that you believe in yourself and the things that you have to say.

Before you can become a hugely influential person, you have to be in a state of pre-influence. This state is when you work on yourself the most, creating an image that people can rely on and trust. During this state of pre-influence, you will have to determine your audience or the people you plan to persuade. Thus, you can better come up with methods of inspiration. For example, if you want to appeal to everyone, what parts of your life might be controversial? If your inspiration is going to be more specific, do you need to improve on certain skills and hobbies? This status of pre-influence will also include bouts of small persuasion when you can really get a good feel for what works and what does not.

How To Master Both Effectively

Consistency is going to be important in mastering both influence and persuasion. If you aren't someone who can be reliable, people are not going to trust you as easily. Humans thrive on consistency. That is why most people work from morning to afternoon, why weekends are free to many, and why many businesses stick to certain hours. When you can be consistent, you can be trusted. If you are not someone who can be trusted, you will not be someone who is influential. Consistency is important in all aspects of influence, so make sure that you aren't sloppy with your methods. If you aren't being consistent with your ways, people will notice that you are trying too hard to influence them.

You have to be someone who people want to hear. If you are nagging others, displaying an attitude that you know what is best, or convincing them using any sort of threat or negativity, people are not going to want to listen to you. If you anger them, it will just drive them away. For instance, many parents have trouble with their teenagers. Teens are at a susceptible stage in their life as they are experimenting with independence and boundaries. When parents put strict rules on their kids and yell at them for doing things that are wrong, the kids usually lose authority, and they end up wanting to do that bad thing their mom or dad told them not to do just to be a little rebellious. To make sure that you are not falling into this trap with anyone, you have to ensure that you are the type of person that others want to hear. Being this type of person comes with respect. Do you respect them? If you don't and instead belittle them, it is going to be harder to get their attention. They might listen to you just to appease you, but if you are too hard on them initially, they will not believe anything that comes out of your mouth.

Start small and build your way to the top. People who try too hard immediately are transparent. If you show that you are desperate to get what you want, it makes you appear as if you don't have your life together, and people will be less likely to become influenced by you. Play it cool no matter how hard that might be. When others see your relaxed attitude, they will be more likely to listen to your methods of persuasion.

Believe in yourself. If you do not buy into what you are saying, people are eventually going to sense it. Do not try to persuade a group of people to do something if you don't undoubtedly think that what you believe is best. Sometimes we are unsure of our own thoughts, and that is fine, but that is not the time when we should be trying to convince others to do something. Influence can be powerful, so if you do something that you are not sure of, it can have serious consequences. Do not be someone who tells people how to live, only to backtrack over your words later and admit that you might have made a mistake. It is easy to change your own mind, but it will not be as easy to undo damage done by misguided influence or persuasion.

Methods of Practice

Persuasion comes from confidence, so if you do not have it in the beginning, it is only going to make it harder to be persuasive later. Do whatever you have to do to grow your confidence. You are going to have to do a lot more than read a book. We have been persuaded to hate our bodies by many different companies in order to profit off our insecurities. People say your hair is too dry, so you buy expensive conditioner. Others will make wrinkles look scary, so you buy expensive ointments to fill the cracks. Remember that you were not born that way; you were taught to hate yourself. Make sure that you exude confidence and know how to have a higher level of self-esteem to make yourself credible. If you don't even believe in what you have to say, why should anyone else?

Look for ways you can persuade people in your daily life. Next time you go shopping at a boutique, practice persuasion by seeing if someone can give you a discount. You can also try going to different garage sales or art shows, as there are opportunities for persuasion there too. Remember that negotiation is important, but it is not interchangeable with persuasion. Instead of improving your negotiation skills, try to see if there are persuasion practices you can use to help you get what you want.

Be careful not to be someone who is becoming too manipulative. It is not about how you can get someone to do something for you. It is more about how you can get them to see things from your perspective so that they want to do it for you. You may persuade someone to do something for you that benefits you a little more sometimes. Remember to find balance. Help others out with your influential abilities as well. Try to convince your boss to not only give you a raise but to help out everyone in your department too. You can have moments where you are a little selfish, but you should never fully take advantage of another person. Just because someone is easily manipulated, it does not mean that we have to take advantage of that quality. Instead, we try to build on their confidence and inspire them to improve from within. It is better that we help people who are more susceptible to persuasion in a positive way before they get wrapped up in a relationship with a narcissist or a psychopath.

Next time you find yourself at the beginning of an argument, stop and take a breath. Instead of fighting, try to figure out how you can persuade someone. It is difficult to keep our emotions under control, and you might have moments where you just want to scream at the other person and tell them that they are wrong. However, screaming is not going to help you on your path to getting what you want. Instead of immediately becoming combative and argumentative, see if there are ways to influence positive change. If you approach them with a neutral attitude, rather than like a soldier fighting a war, they are more likely to buy into your ideas and openness for discussion.

Now, let's delve deeper into the principles and core qualities of both persuasion and influence that you will need to find success.

Chapter 10 Mind Reading

Mind reading is a very controversial subject brought into disrepute by the many charlatans, suspense films and television dramas that depict this as some sort of mysterious dark art. For the purposes of this publication, it may be better to think in terms of emotional or mood interpretation. In fact, science is only now beginning to get to grips with our ability if not to mind read, then at least to be able to interpret the feelings and emotions of others. It has recently been discovered that we have an area within our brains that actively tries to replicate the emotion of people we are interacting with.

In basic terms, we are observing others and attempting to walk in their emotional shoes in a figurative way. This is nothing new and most of us practice it to a certain extent in our day-to-day lives. Children are able to interpret when their parents are angry while a husband may know his wife is feeling unwell even if she has not voiced any complaint. This emotional recognition is normally generated because we are dealing with someone with whom we are very familiar but the skills can be developed to work with anyone if we are open to trying and willing to put in the time to do so. It is an unfortunate indictment of our fast-paced lives that we have lost much of this talent, simply because we are so often in such a hurry that we don't use this ability anymore.

A good place to start is a person's facial expression. We often wear our mood on our faces, and if you make an effort to observe someone carefully then you will gain a good deal of information about the way they are feeling. Of course, the moment we detect we are being observed we try to disguise our emotions, and so it's necessary to hide the fact that you are watching someone. Never study their face for more than a few seconds at a time but do so deliberately and with the intention of assessing their mood. As you practice this, you will find you become better at it. At the same time, notice their body language but only to confirm what you are reading in their face. I always say "focus on the context, not on the content": notice how they're moving, how they're standing, how they're using their bodies, simply because body language never lies. This amalgamation of physical displays, though quite unintentional on the part of the person displaying them, will help you develop a better understanding of that person at any given time.

Once you have taken the time to get to know a person and have started to have a better understanding of how they function in both an emotional and physical way, more insights will become obvious. If a person becomes withdrawn, perhaps there is some sort of problem. If a person is more gregarious and loud, perhaps he's trying to impress someone or angling for a promotion.

It is hard to overstate the benefits of just watching the people with whom you interact. In every way, you should be developing your ability to quietly detach yourself from your environment and observe. This will teach you all sorts of things about a person and the group dynamics that surround you. All of this is vital information that you will be able to use to your own benefit when the time is right for you to make persuasive moves.

Some of the information you glean from your study of people will just be filed away for use at a later stage. Other information should be acted upon perhaps to build relationships. If you detect, for example, that one of your work colleagues is depressed then at an appropriate time perhaps you should gently ask a few questions. Remember to remain sensitive and empathetic, but by putting yourself in a position to give the emotional support you are building a bridge. If things go well, you will have someone at your back when it comes time to use your persuasive powers, and this is important from a number of angles.

- When you put forward a suggestion, you already have someone that is likely to support you.

- You have started, therefore, to develop a group dynamic that others will lean toward.

- Hopefully, as a result of your intervention, he perceives you as trustworthy.

- The person is likely to say positive things about you that will increase your credibility.

- That person has a feeling of indebtedness toward you that he's anxious to repay.

All in all, by reading their emotional state you will develop a better understanding of their behavioral patterns that will prove useful to you at some later stage. Providing you act on that gleaned information with the correct attitude and at the appropriate time, the benefits can be enormous and all at the cost of just stepping back and observing for a few minutes. The more you understand them, the better your chances of persuading them to follow your leadership at some time in the future.

Chapter 11 The Persuasive Power Of Fear

The Mechanism of Fear

Fear is an extremely powerful tool that has been used and abused by ruthless people for years. Fear is not a pleasant emotion, but is one of the most powerful using the threat of danger, pain or harm.

Fear is most commonly said to be one of the human passions. Some psychologist considers it to be the passion the most contrary to love. We would usually say that hatred is opposed to love. But don't we hate the most the persons who we used to love and who have hurt us so badly that our love has turned to hatred? The fear operates differently. It is as if fear and love exclude one another. We fear only what is contrary to what we love. As love regards good, so fear regards evil. More precisely, it observes a representation of a future evil.

Fear relates to evil as overcoming some particular good. This future evil is more powerful than the person who fears it. That's why we perceive it is arduous and difficult to avoid. What we fear is to lose what we love and possess or not to obtain what we are hoping for. When we love somebody or something that is good for us, and then we become deprived of that good, we consider it to be an evil act. It is precisely such an evil that fear regards.

As we have said, fear arouses from the imagination or the representation of certain threatening evil which is difficult to overcome. The difficulty in repelling the dreaded evil comes from the greatness of the evil and the weakness of him who fears. The smaller power, the lesser influence. And the contrary holds as well: the bigger the power, the greater influence. That's why we fear the powerful people, in particular when they are unjust or opposed to us.

It is worthwhile to note that, since fear is aroused by an imagination of the future evil, that the one who takes away the imagination, he also takes away the fear.

There is a gradation in fear. Fear increases in proportion with an increase of evil that is feared. It seems that among different circumstances which affect our representation of fear, the one that does it the most is the time. We fear more the things that last long then the ones that last only a short period of time.

Examples of Fear

Many leaders and tyrants have understood the power of fear and have used it as a method to control others for their own benefit. Fear is contagious and, if used ruthlessly, it has immense power to persuade people to proceed along paths they may not normally have taken. Although this dynamic is most obvious when used by military and political tyrants, it can often be seen to a lesser extent being used in corporate, religious, family or marital environments.

The sheer power of the fear mechanism, when used by those ruthless enough to do so, can be enormous. It should not only be seen in a negative light as it can be incredibly productive when harnessed correctly. An example may be the results that a team of workers can come up with, when under the fear of not meeting a deadline.

The person who uses this method of persuasion needs to be extremely cautious, however. Fear produces a fight-or-flight reaction and is not often conducive to true loyalty. Sure, you may be able to encourage a team to rush off and produce incredible results when under pressure. Understand, though, they are going to resent having been placed under this pressure, and when the time comes that they feel they should fight, then you had better be watching your own back... because there is not likely to be anyone there to watch it for you.

As a tool, fear has its place, but those who choose it as the main weapon in their armory often find that they lead from a lonely position, as the only loyalty comes from those whom they are most able to intimidate. People may follow out of fear, but they will resent the person who causes that fear. The result is usually short term gain, which disintegrates when the fear dissipates. This means that constant stress has to be applied to the people being intimidated, or the whole relationship will fall apart.

Conversely building loyalty may not show the same short term benefits as it requires much more effort, time and vulnerability on the part of those attempting to build it. It also needs a higher level of trust between both parties or groups, but when properly developed creates a far stronger and more enduring bond. It also allows for greater input from all parties, which can produce a wider more all-encompassing result. This contrast between developing fear or developing loyalty is something you will need to weigh up in your own relationships and the persuasive tactics you choose to pursue.

That said, fear can be used in other ways as well. You do not always need to induce fear of your power or influence, but play on the emotional fears of others.

This tactic is most evident in the cosmetic and beauty industry. Many beauty companies are built on the premise of their consumer's fear of aging or looking imperfect. They dish out everything from anti-aging creams to zit removers to help men and women get rid of their imperfections, yet fear mongering is dripping from their advertisements. Diet supplements and weight loss products is also another sector of the beauty industry that plays on people's fear. They instill the fear of gaining weight and not having the body of a model, while playing on the fear of what health conditions can arise for people who are overweight.

You see, fear affects our perception of ourselves, as well as those around us. It changes our view to make even the most harmless of things into frightful or concerning objects we wish to avoid. Fear does not need to be extreme or crippling either. It just needs to be something which people are concerned about. Some employees might be fearful of doing a bad job. Now, you can play on your employee's fear, and naturally, instill the idea of how doing a certain act would lead to bad performance. This fear can be positive.

Fear should still be used sparingly at most. In fact, if you use it often, fear would either cause too much anxiety and paralysis or lose its effect. If you want to learn what type and how much fear you want to apply, get to know people better. Find the right amount and apply it with the lightest touch, and you will have yourself a powerful tool at your disposal.

Chapter 12 Ten Ways To Positively Influence Others In Your Workplace

It doesn't matter how hard you work or how brilliant you are, you cannot succeed in anything without cooperation from other people. We are not only individuals; we are all connected to one another in some way. The world is actually shrinking as, at the touch of a button, the click of a mouse, we can keep up with and keep in contact with even the most remote parts of our globe, and we can learn from other cultures as easily as we learn from our own. No matter which part of the world we come from, we are not so different. We all have the same needs, as does any stranger that we meet. The same thing can also be said about the people that we work with.

It doesn't matter where you work, and it doesn't matter what you do for a living. We all have one thing in common – a large part of our waking hours are spent in our workplaces, some of us in jobs that we like and some in jobs that we hate.

If you are the latter, if you are working at a place or doing a job that you simply don't like, you can make your life much more bearable by persuading people to be on your side. You might even find that you quite enjoy going to work after all.

Here are 10 ways that you can positively influence other people in your workplace and make life so much easier to bear:

Be Grateful

Or at least get into the habit of being grateful. Before you leave home every morning, look around at what you have and say the words "thank you." Be thankful that you have a home, maybe a car, food on the table and a family to share it with. Once you learn to appreciate what you have, your purpose will become much clearer – to bring home the money to pay for it all, the money that the job you hate pays you every week or month. As the day goes on and you face challenges that seem insurmountable, reflect on your gratefulness. It will make you happier, and it will make it easier for you to carry on.

Be Happy

Happiness truly is contagious, and there are, in all truthfulness, more than a billion reason to be happy. We weren't put on the earth to be miserable, so find a reason to be happy. Rejoice in the sky, the sun, the rain that gives life. Talk to your colleagues, the people who help you through each day at work; smile at those who don't help you. If you are alive and healthy, then you are doing okay. If you are happy others will be happy too.

Keep on Smiling

Even if you don't feel like it. There is an old expression, "fake it until you make it" and it has never been truer, especially when things go wrong. No matter what is happening, no matter how bad you feel - smile, and you will feel better. If the boss is on your back, your co-workers are not pulling their weight, your computer crashed and wiped out everything you did, just smile. There is actually a scientific reason for it: smiling helps to release endorphins in the blood, and these are not called happy hormones for nothing. Smiling also eases tension, not just in you but in those around you as well. People will notice, they will begin smiling, and the tension will ease. You and you alone will have persuaded everyone that everything is ok, with just a smile. A powerful way to smile is to look up at the ceiling while opening your arms and your chest. This simple move will increase your testosterone level and will boost your mood.

Always Say Your Pleases and Thank Yous

Good manners get you a long way and help to build up better relationships. This isn't just about the workplace, this works anywhere you go, to a restaurant, the movies, the grocery store. Be polite and show manners and people will do what they can to help you. In the workplace, your colleagues will more be likely to help you out if you are polite and treat them with the respect and courtesy you expect from them. Good manners show that you care so make it a habit of treating others as you want to be treated.

Steer Clear of the Gossip

At any given moment of the day, something will be happening in your workplace that gives people a reason to talk, to gossip about someone else behind their back. It is human nature to talk about things that happen, but the nature of gossip is that it often becomes distorted, purely for entertainment value. Gossip is demoralizing to the subject, and it can also be classed as bullying if it turns malicious. If you happen to be in a place where people are gossiping, and they try to draw you in, just smile at them and then walk away. Show them you will not become involved and avoid the negativity. Not only does it keep you stabilized, but it will also stop you from, wrongly, judging the victim and will also gain you respect from others.

Be Nice to the "Village Idiot."

It doesn't matter where you work, there will always be the "village idiot." This is perhaps a very cruel term because the victim of that term is, more often than not, merely eccentric, different from others, not so articulate. It doesn't make them an actual idiot. Whenever you have cause to speak to them, be nice to them, listen to what they have to say, and you might just be surprised at how un-idiot like they actually are. Too often, we label people unfairly and, by taking the tie to include them, to listen to them, you are developing a large amount of good will. You don't know when you may need to call on people for help, so make sure you keep them on your side.

Be Diplomatic

Everywhere you go, there will be people who say or do things that cause irritation. The real key is to stay objective and to stay calm. Losing your temper, or choosing to be angry as your very first reaction will do nothing more than providing the fire with a much-needed fuel source to keep on irritating you. Allow it to happen, and your colleagues will lose all respect for you. It doesn't matter how hard it is not to respond, when people say things that are hurtful or simply irritating, do not respond. Remain in control, remain calm, and you will be left alone. If you can muster one, smile at them and then continue with what you were doing. And if you do have to say something, keep your voice soft and be kind to them. It is your anger that they want, and if you don't give it, they have nothing. You, on the other hand, will gain the respect of your colleagues. Always be non-reactive.

Do Your Very Best All of the Time

Your bosses and any colleagues who are influential will respect you more if you always do the very best that you can. Even if you are at odds with people, doing your best, putting in your effort, will result in milestones being reached and deadline met. People may not like you for one reason or another, but they can still respect you for being someone they can depend on, someone who remains focused. You will also have a better sense of self-worth and purpose. It may result in a raise or promotion, or it could just mean that you are in a better position to influence others in the future.

Always Be Honest

Honesty is always the very best policy, and when you add diplomacy into the mix, you have the makings of a great communicator, a true leader. When you are trying to talk to others about your ideas, keep to the facts; don't throw in a lot of technical jargon and don't try to be too smart – it will backfire on you. Never exaggerate your claim, and never embellish them as people can see through that and your chances of persuading them round to your way of thinking will be gone. It isn't always the contents of the message that work; it is the way the message is conveyed.

Respect Other Cultures

The world is multicultural and, no matter where you live and work, you will come across people of different ethnicities and different cultures. Get to know them, get to know their traditions, beliefs, food choices and develop respect for them. Each different ultra has something that we can all learn from, and it is our moral duty to show them respect. Walk away from racist conversations; if you stay, if you join in, you are no better than they are. Having that kind of name does not help you to be able to influence others, and everyone will lose a little of their respect for you. No matter where you go, no matter which nationalities you come across there will be good people and bad.

Focus your energies on the good in all of us, and you will find that people are more prepared to cooperate with you, to follow where you want to lead them.

These may not seem like ways to persuade people but think about everything I have said carefully. By being nice to others, showing respect and remaining calm and dependable, you are turning yourself into someone that others will trust in, that they will want to follow. This is an essential part of powerful leadership.

Chapter 13 Undetectable Mind Control

The truth can be a destroyer of illusions. This is why it can be hard to hear, and you can use this fact to your advantage. You have heard about the law of attraction. If you think it, you attract it. That is the basic premise. Now, whether this works or not remains unseen, but you can modify this tactic to make it work for you and your ability to persuade others.

The first step is making sure that you have full control over your mind. This allows you to think efficiently and gain a greater understanding of how the human mind works. It is imperative that you understand this before you can control the mind of another person without being detected. The following tips will help you to gain control over your own mind first:

Deal with the troubles in your mind and sort them out.

Go into controlling your mind with a plan.

When working on this, be calm because it ensures an open mind.

Still your visceral responses.

Relax your muscles.

Utilize breathing exercises and meditation to get deeper into your own mind.

Sense the physical symptoms that come with your thoughts.

Evaluate all of your thoughts for a source and reason.

Once you do this, you will know what all of your thoughts mean, and you can control them. Once you master controlling your own mind, you will be able to seamlessly transfer over to controlling the minds of others without being detected.

Mind Control in Society

You see mind control every day and you have even fallen victim to it. The majority of it is used in advertising and marketing. For example, you see a television commercial that really captures your attention. The product is not one you absolutely need, but the commercial captured your mind and essentially told you on a subconscious level that you need the product. So, you go and buy it. You had no idea your mind was being controlled. In fact, you probably did not realize it until reading this section right now.

When you master undetectable mind control, you will essentially be marketing yourself. The end result will not be others buying you but giving you what you want.

Undetectable Mind Control Techniques

There are several techniques that you will use when you are working to control the minds of others. All of these are relatively simple to implement once you have gained control over your own mind. The following are effective undetectable mind control techniques to learn:

Think for them: When you need something from someone, do not give them a chance to think it over. Tell them what they are thinking and what they are going to do. People are naturally busy and if you ask them to consider something, they are likely to either forget or not give it enough thought to give you your desired outcome. When you help them not have to think, they view it as you helping them, making them more likely to give you what you want.

Ask for an inch: When you are assessing how easy a person is to control, you want to take baby steps so that they never catch on to what you are doing. So, start with small things first, such as asking them to buy you a drink or making them take you to a movie. From here, you can persuade them to do larger things, such as paying a bill for you or buying you something on the pricey side. It is all about testing the waters and essentially priming your target.

Give some too: If all you do is take, no matter how naïve a person is, they are going to eventually catch on to what you are doing. So, on occasion, buy them a drink, give them a compliment or offer to pay for the movie. This makes the relationship seem balanced and even, but what you are actually doing is ensuring that they continue to be available for whatever you need from them.

Instill fear: You essentially want to set up a situation that makes the person feel afraid. When people are afraid they are easier to control and make suggestions to.

Instill guilt: Make the person feel guilty and they will be putty in your hands. The key here is to alleviate your guilt and reverse the roles as seamlessly as possible. This is a great mind control technique for those that are harder to break with other methods. Once you cause them to feel guilt for what they perceive is something bad happening to you, immediately act and make suggestions to get what you want from them since guilt goes away quickly when induced this way.

Chapter 14 Influence Through Seduction

The whole point of seduction is to make someone want you. The motive is usually to cause someone to become sexually attracted to you. Seduction is one of the most powerful persuasion techniques because you are persuading someone to give their entire selves to you. There are multiple seduction tips and techniques that you can use. No matter who you are or who the person is who you are trying to seduce, these methods will work. What is ideal about them is that they do not require much preparation, so you can really start using them right now.

Choose the Right Person

You can seduce anyone, but you will put in less effort when you choose wisely. Look for a person who tends to be shy and reserved. They tend to be more vulnerable and in need of a person's attention. When you start giving them attention, it is easy to seduce them to take it to the next level.

Send Mixed Signals

This is a seduction technique that is as old as time. People feel challenged when they are getting mixed signals. A challenge automatically makes a person more interested in winning the prize, which in this case is you.

Create a Need

Make it to where the person you are trying to seduce feels like they need you. You can make this need purely sexual or make it deeper than that. When you create a need, it creates feeling of discontent and anxiety, both of which are more likely to make a person keep pursuing you.

False Sense of Security

When a person feels secure with you, this automatically creates a bond. This makes it easier to persuade them to give you what you want. This security is false, but by the time they figure this out, you will have what you have wanted.

Make Yourself Desirable

People do not like to lose. They do not like seeing other people with a person they are interested in. Once you hook someone, force them to see you with other people who also are interested in you. This creates an uneasiness that forces them to make their move because they will fear that they will lose you.

Create Temptation

No one likes to be tempted to something and then not be able to have it. This is true for everything from food, to career to romantic relationships. When you tempt the person, but then stop them once they are on the edge, this essentially drives them crazy. When a person is in this frame of mind, you can pretty much get whatever it is that you want.

Utilize Suspense

You want to give them some attention, but not your full attention. Just like when you create temptation, this is going to put them into a hyper-competitive state. You are going to be the only person that they think about. Their thoughts of you are going to filter into all elements of their lives. This is what you want, because at this stage, you have full control.

Be Mysterious

People love mystery. It draws them in and they want to do everything that they can to solve it. When you create mystery, you will naturally seduce those that become curious. The key is to give some information but hold back the juiciest details. Now, the mystery can be about anything really. However, avoid talking about an ex since this can have the opposite effect on someone you are trying to seduce. Other ways to add mystery include good eye contact, putting the attention back on them when they ask questions, smiling a lot and always speaking in a neutral tone.

Subtly Make Yourself Stand Out

You do not want it to be obvious that you are trying to get their attention. Instead, you want it to seem like you stand out just because of who you are. For example, women can wear red lipstick because this is not uncommon, but it still makes you stand out. Men can have the same effect with a bright or patterned tie. The key is to choose one small element that will make you stand out against the crowd that is relatively natural.

Utilize Scents

Did you know that the scent of a person can be all that it takes to attract another person? Now, all people have their own preferred scents, so it is a good idea to get to know a bit about the person and their preferences before you use this technique. Scent has a subconscious type of influence. It gives people information about another person without them even realizing it, so it is one of the subtlest and effective ways to up your seduction progress.

Be Mindful of Your Assets

Physical attraction is obviously a major element when it comes to seduction. However, you do not want to show off all of the goods because this can have a negative effect. For example, men with strong arms might wear a short-sleeved shirt. This way the person they are trying to seduce can see this asset without it being too obvious that they are trying to show off. Women might wear a form-fitting dress that hits below the knee and covers the chest well. In this case, you are covered, but the person you are trying to seduce can still see your full figure.

Confuse Them

One time you see them, give them all of your attention, but the next, only give them partial attention. This confusion ups their thinking of you and it makes you more mysterious and desirable. Just make sure that there is a good balance here or else you might actually turn the other person off.

Be Bold

Once you are ready to go in for the kill, you want to be bold. You have already hooked them at this point and they are yours to do with as you please. So, there is no reason to wait for them to make a move. Just grab the moment and make it known what you want.

Chapter 15 How To Convince Someone Of Your Opinion

When you find yourself needing to convince someone of your opinion, you are already in a conflict situation. Most people would rather do anything but be found conflicting. They would rather bite their tongues even when they know they are right, rather than put forward conflicting ideas and have to waste their strength arguing about it. It takes courage to speak up because it demonstrates your insight and your value to a team. If you choose not to speak up, you risk being branded as ineffective and redundant, and this could be the end of your career, friendship, marriage, and other social associations.

Most of us fear to express our opinions because we perceive that it will lead to an engaging tedious battle of opinion. The reality is that persuasion is all about telling someone what he wants to hear to be convinced. When you want to persuade, do not begin by blatantly expressing your controversial opinion, start by first considering what your audience wants, taking yourself out of the equation, and focus on connecting with your audience on the topic.

How to Persuade

Whenever you have a valid point of disagreement, nothing should keep you from expressing your opinion. However, if you need to be heard, go about it with some form of decorum so that you know what to say, how to say it, and when to say it. Here are a few guidelines to help you through it:

1. Choose Your Battles

If you walked a mile asking the people you met to give their opinions and views about a particular topic, the chances are that you would find quite a number who would disagree with you. The issues could range from trivial matters such as how to press the toothpaste tube to serious matters like disciplining kids. In almost all issues of life, expect some opposition. People will not always agree with you, and you do not have to conflict with them every time.

You cannot afford to go fighting or to argue with people everywhere. That would wreck your social life and even deny your inner peace. Instead, choose to ignore the trivial issues and only focus on the things that matter. When you do this, even those around you will respect you. You have very limited social capital- how much of it are you willing to risk on conflicts because you insist on speaking your mind all the time?

Always think before you engage with others, and weigh the situation to see whether the issue at hand is worth your attention. Most of the time, it does not.

2. Give It Some Thought

When you have thought about the issue and felt that you need to speak up, be silent and rethink your position. Are you sure that you want to take that position on the matter? Is that the right thing to do? Are there any supporting facts?

Having these thoughts will keep you from jumping on to a topic with minimal information and embarrassing yourself. Giving your ideas a second thought will also ensure that you have all the facts straight, and where needed, you may even change your mind. You could also realize that the issue in question is not worth your time, and you may give up on the issue entirely.

3. Avoid Being So Emotional

It is risky to get into an argument or confrontation when you are overly anxious, angry or resentful; doing it will get you spewing venom you would regret. Your counterparts will also be provoked to become harsh and unreasonable, and in the end, you will have prompted the situation to escalate to a massive issue while it could have been resolved rationally.

If you want to get the respect of your peers, your seniors and your juniors, stick to reason and only engage a reasonable amount of emotion in your undertakings. If you are always reactive to situations and handle your issues led by emotions, you will appear irresponsible, and people will not want to be around you.

If a situation aggravates or excites you too much, take a step back, take some deep breaths, relax and stay calm so that you can address people respectfully.

4. Ensure That You Are Not Making Things Worse

Sometimes you want to find a solution to a problem by putting your views across, but you end up making things worse. It happens to us all. However, the frequency of this happening will lower if you purpose to engage only in conversations and arguments that will lead to something productive. Stay away from idle talk that is meant to bring people down.

5. Do Not Insist on Your Way All the Time

Some people go by the erroneous 'my way or the highway' philosophy. Thinking that you are always right, but others are wrong is a sign of pride. Only a person who is so full of himself, a narcissist, will think that he is always right and cannot make mistakes.

Instead, you should pass your views as opinions to be considered rather than as the final decisions. Doing this will more likely produce a favorable response from your audience compared to imposing your will on them. The moment you force the other party to take a defensive position, know that you blew it already.

6. Let the Facts Lead

Your opinion is an opinion like that of any other individual, and it is based on your intuition and the information you have so far. Others around you could also have influenced your stand on any particular issue. For these reasons, opinions are quite subjective. Therefore, while you need to speak confidently about what you think, ensure that you stick to the merits of your position, and back them up with data and statistics.

7. Allow the Other Side A Chance

Your opinion, even when it is right, does not have to carry the day. There could be bits about the other side's view that could build on your ideas. Therefore, as you argue out your point, come up with creative ways to incorporate the other party's opinions too. Give support to their ideas and way of reasoning, and you will see that they will start to be friendlier and accommodating of your opinions too.

Methods of Persuasion

Below is a brief discussion of methods you can use to persuade someone to take up your ideas:

1. Questions

The questioning method is used to grasp the attention of your audience. When asked a question in a discussion, people begin to think about the appropriate answer to the question, and they also wonder the reason you asked them that particular question. However, you ought to be careful and to only ask questions that will add to your discussion because undoubtedly, your audience's minds will waver as they think of the right response to give. To get the right results, ensure that the questions you ask are short, simple, and logical. Let the questions inspire deeper thinking rather than taking away the audience's attention from your discussion.

2. Repetition

Repetition serves to incite and improve your brain's retention power. Once something is repeated to you, the odds of it getting stuck to your memory increase. Ensure that the sentences you speak highlight the keywords you want your audience to remember, and make an effort to repeat the most significant sentences or words. Place them strategically, and where possible, have your audience repeat them out loud, or put them down on paper.

3. Use Simulations

This is an excellent method for convincing strangers because you have not related before, and you cannot say anything about their mental abilities. You cannot also predict how they will react to certain statements, especially when discussing controversial issues. Using simulations creates an analogy by taking out the names of real places, people, and other things that could distract the listener and take his mind away from the subject.

For example, if you want to convince a college dropout to return to school, avoid mentioning places and names that could change the course of your discussion and shift it in an unfavorable direction. Do not mention the names of people that dropped out of school and succeeded like Bill Gates or Mark Zuckerberg. Do not also mention the names of people that dropped out of college and failed. Your aim should be to convince your audience, based on the unique circumstances that getting back in college would be the best decision he can make.

When you stick to the student's unique circumstances, he is likely to reflect on the reasons you gave and find some inspiration to finish his education. Giving examples of what other people did does not help much, what would help him is drawing the inspiration from within when times get difficult, rather from other people's stories. Sure, mentorship is a useful motivator, but the spirit in a man is what keeps him pushing and motivated, not the experiences of others.

4. Refute the Opinions of Others

Refuting can be difficult for many people, especially for those who hate or fear confrontations. It is also challenging because it requires a person to pay close attention to the opinions the other person has expressed, break it into smaller ideas, and then go about disapproving every one of them. Once you have knocked all of them down, now present your opinion and show how it is the better opinion. It is crucial that you rely on logic and reason throughout this process and present compelling facts that the other person knows about. That way, the other person will see the logic in your ideas and take them up.

As you present your ideas, the most important thing to do is to ensure that you have proof of your opinions. Of course, some beliefs cannot be proven, such as the question of taste (you cannot say you are right for finding an ice cream flavor sweeter than the other), because neither opinion could be wrong. However, in matters where you can provide proof, be sure to provide it.

Facts give the illusion that what you are saying is accurate and irrefutable. Therefore, when trying to convince people to take up your opinion, persuade them that it is a fact, even when it is not. Sadly, sometimes people twist the facts, but this is not something you should be engaging in.

Manipulators convince you that their opinions are better than yours by first getting into your head to see what you already know. Many of them will get you talking, and as you go on and on, they will be collecting information, wanting to see just how much you know.

From there, the manipulator cleverly repeats the facts you just stated back to you, adding in some more details. You will think that you are adding to your knowledge, but the truth is that these facts may not even be real. The manipulator might be making them up or twisting information to favor them. You see, there are very many ways to manipulate information. Some people, instead of agreeing with what you know, will go the other way and begin to discrediting what you know by presenting it as faulty. They do this by bending the facts a bit or presenting new crafted facts to the table. You end up denying the truth you already knew and taking up erroneous information. By the time you realize it, the person will have gotten away with much.

Chapter 16 How To Stop Fearing Judgment

You notice someone stealing a glance in your direction, look the other way, whisper to a friend, and they burst out laughing.

What will you think?

If you have social anxiety, like many of us do, you will assume that the duo is laughing at you. Your logical part of the brain will tell you that they are laughing about something else. Which side will you believe? The best thing to do is to ignore the socially anxious, insecure part of your brain. It is always better to assume that the people are not bothered about you because most times, it's true.

Despite what society and your very own mind tell you, the reality is that the majority of the people around us are nice. Even if their thoughts of you are negative, they rarely will say anything, let alone laugh in your presence. Even if they did, do not allow their behavior to affect you.

While you may already know this, that people are rarely bothered by what you do, why do you continue to fear what people might say or think about you? Why do you fear judgment?

The fear of judgment is rooted in fear of 'not being enough.' It comes about when people feel unlovable and unworthy. Those who judge others are drawing from the same. They project their sense of insecurity to others because their energy is focused on the external rather than internal condition. They get some short-lived relief from judging others, and to prolong the experience; they result in judging anything and everything around them. For some, judging turns into an addiction, and they can't help it. It makes them feel better and somewhat validated. Fortunately, the proportion that is interested in judging others for self-gratification is tiny.

While outside influences are only a small proportion, their influence on the rest of the people is felt profoundly. They influence the words, perception and the attitude a person has about himself. Quickly, after listening to the small group's ideas and opinions, an individual becomes his harshest critic. They fail to understand that when you judge yourself, you get stuck in emotions like fear, shame, resentment, anger and comparison rather than experience the love, joy, peace, compassion, happiness, and appreciation that comes with valuing and accepting yourself.

Taking Hollywood for example, the construct of what beauty is must have been the erroneous idea of only a few people, but today, people have taken up that belief, and they continue to hold themselves to nearly impossible standards of beauty. People now starve themselves, take up dangerous surgeries, or continue to put foreign items in their bodies in their quest to fit the bill of what has been said to be beautiful. The result has been a population working to look like the Kardashian/Jenner clan, Angelina Jolie, Brad Pitt and other people who are thought to be beautiful. Sadly, they don't see that they were beautiful, because everyone is.

Without knowledge of how to beat the fear of judgment, a person can go through life with many problems. However, the following points can help you get a grip on your fear:

1. Identify Your Strengths and Limitations

If you are already aware of your strong points and your weak ones, people, with their judgments, are less likely to affect you. Even if they were to gossip or comment on your weak points, you would already be aware of it, and it would hurt less than if you had been living in denial. Therefore, let your strengths guide you towards increasing your confidence, and be aware of your weaknesses better than other people. If anyone says anything about you, tell them that you are aware of the shortcomings.

You see, when someone comes at you telling you of your weaknesses, or even telling others about them, his or her intention is to pull you down. They hope to get you by surprise, embarrass you and possibly even crush your spirit. However, when you are aware of your weak areas, you will not be moved when bad things are said about you. Their judgments and impressions will be irrelevant.

Always remember that you are a unique person and that it is the combination of both the strengths and the weaknesses in you that culminates to the awesome person you are. They make up your character and individuality. They are therefore essential, and you need to own them all.

That said, if there are things about your character that you can change, kindly work on that. Do not own up to nasty qualities like rudeness, impatience, and other similar attributes. However, own up to the other natural characteristics that you have no control over.

2. Do Not Allow Others to Define You

If you listened to them, you would realize that people always have an opinion. What's worse, they never take a stand: what is cool to them about you today, tomorrow they will dislike. If they had their way, you would be like the chameleon, constantly changing to suit their changing opinions. What a miserable life that would be! If you want to live a peaceful, happy life, why would you give attention to people's opinions even for a moment?

One thing you must understand is that the people are entitled to an opinion. You cannot keep them from thinking and generating ideas, even when they are about you. However, you can lower the impact that other people's ideas and opinions have on you by working on your self-confidence and self-esteem. It might be difficult to do that, but it starts with coming to terms with what you feel about yourself and beginning to work on areas of your character that you can change. Work on your strengths and magnify them, so that they overshadow the weaknesses you cannot change.

3. Take Charge of The Inner Critic

The inner voice in you can get quite brutal sometimes. It leads you to say to yourself harsh words that others cannot even tell you, and you cannot say to others. Therefore, the first step, when you want to get rid of the self-doubt, self-sabotage, and fear of judgment, is to silence that inner critic and the negative thoughts it produces. The values, beliefs, ethnicity, and age of a person do not contribute to the challenges in a person's life as much as the negative voices in the person's head.

Knowing the damage that negative thoughts bring to your life is an important drive towards your improvement of the beliefs you carry about yourself. It drives you to want to regain back control of your thoughts and beliefs about yourself, and once you have done that, you begin to make changes to your thinking, adopting a more positive outlook on life, and becoming more optimistic and positive. You do not have to worry about what people think about you either.

4. Prioritize Your Life and Your Self

Whenever you allow another person's opinion of you to cloud your perception of you, you have already prioritized that person and his or her thoughts concerning you. You have given that person the power to influence all other issues that affect you.

If someone says that you are not fun to be around, for example, you are likely to keep off friends and social groups so that others do not also confirm that you are boring to be around. You do not want to dampen their day with your presence. However, by cutting off your social life, you will be putting yourself at a disadvantage because you will not be interacting, sharing thoughts, and having fun with other people. Slowly, your life will become duller and duller, and the malicious negative person's comments will have wrecked your social life.

If after the comment, you decide to take the other route and decide to prove to everyone that you are a fun person, you are up for an uphill task. You may be forced to go out more often, drink more than you usually do, interact with people you typically would not and do a bunch of other out-of-character activities to prove that you are fun. By the time you get tired of it, you will have wasted money you would have put into something productive, taken on habits that you wouldn't otherwise, and interacted with people that you would be better off keeping off.

Neither of these scenarios compares to what would be the case had the decision to engage in more fun activities been born out of your desires. You would have moved at your own pace, and not engaged in anything out of character. You would have pulled back if you came to levels you were not willing to get into because you wouldn't be trying to prove anything. That is the advantage of moving at your own pace, rather than following the will and advice of others.

You must accept that you are the expert of your life, and no one knows you better than you know yourself. You are fully aware of your capabilities because you know what you are good at and what you struggle with. You trust yourself, and you wouldn't intentionally do things that would harm you. Own up to the issues in your life, and let go of all that does not benefit. Prioritize your opinion and your needs, and do not allow another to take control of your life, or to influence the feelings you have about yourself.

5. Invest in Yourself

For the issues and parts of life, you wish to have some assistance with, get the support you need. Ensure that all you do in life is directly contributing to your growth and wellbeing. Work towards becoming happier every day by doing more of what you find fun. Of course, some things that are good for you will not be much fun at first, such as going for a daily run, but with time, you will get used to it. Do things that will help you overcome personal challenges too. If anything, ensure that you are living your best life daily.

Conclusion

Persuasion is one of the most important aspects of communication. It is necessary to convince others to listen to you in order to get them to work for you. To help you develop and hone your persuasion skills, this book should provide you with ample material designed to get you started on the right foot.

To start off, it's wise to understand the 6 basic principles or "weapons" of persuasion Cialdini describes, especially if you are in a commercial or marketing environment. They will help you understand the basic human psychological tendencies in behavior when it comes to influence and identify when you can employ them into your own situation. These principles have been tried and tested and accepted universally.

All human beings are motivated by one aspect of life or another. According to John Maslow, humans tend to follow a hierarchy when it comes to attaining life's goals. Understanding this hierarchy can help you lead a better life. Once you are aware of these basic physical and psychological motivators you will be able to assess people much more efficiently and have a better idea of what they may respond to.

There are different types of persuasion techniques that can be used to influence others and each one is applicable in a particular situation. All of them are based on theories that have either been tested through scientific study, my own personal experience and many times a combination of both. These include tactics such as "Reversal Tagging/Counter-Attitudinal Advocacy/Anchoring/Hurt and Rescue" just to name a few. Understanding them and using them in your daily life can help control situations to a certain extent and persuading others to listen to you. But consistency of application will be key and practice essential.

There will be many different situations that will arise in your day-to-day life where you will be required to use persuasion techniques. Being aware of these situations will prepare you to respond in a manner that will turn it around for you and work in your favor.

My life has been filled with high-pressure situations of all descriptions and in order to stay in control and remain in command of them, I had to make use of a certain skill set that supersedes normal and everyday discourse. Your communication needs to be crystal clear; you need to be well prepared having done your homework. You also need to be adaptable and while all of the time controlling your emotions. These skills should be developed as they are not inherently present in everyone. However with a little dedication and effort in the right direction, you will be able to develop and hone these skills so you can handle these high stakes situations when they come around.

It is no secret that everybody loves a charismatic personality, gravitas is difficult to defeat when it comes to the persuasion game. So you must try to develop your charms and use your personality to influence others where ever you can. There are certain basic personality enhancing elements to develop that will guide you through the process of persuasion such as improving vocal expressions and gestures, dressing the part and becoming a great story teller. Developing a strong personality can, in fact, make it extremely easy to influence others, as half the work will be taken care of for you.

Small talk is another important skill to develop in life. It's the glue in the fabric of conversations that allow you to move seamlessly from topic to topic. It also allows you the opportunity to talk with complete strangers or garner information you otherwise wouldn't have gotten. You must engage in small talk with everyone and anywhere you go. Keep it as interesting as possible and with time and practice, it will become progressively easier to carry out and your conversations will be exponentially more fruitful as a result.

When it comes to high level communication it is important to maintain the right type of language when you come in contact with people. What you say will say a lot about you, so make sure your vocabulary is broad and strong enough to stand the test. It's not always about good or impressive language either, it is equally important to taper what you are saying to the current audience. Use the lexicon and phrases they would use. Also never underestimate the impact of impeccable greeting and goodbyes. These are the things that people will remember the most so don't waste them with weak introductions or forgetting people's names.

It takes a lot of conscious skill and effort to be a good listener, to really indulge in what somebody is saying in a mindful manner. The majority of us do not take up this opportunity to learn what the other person is really telling us as we are either too easily distracted by things around us or simply just waiting for our term to talk. You need to really focus in to what the other person is saying and picking up on the details. This was one of my biggest weapons as a spy. Without realizing it, people tend to give away important information that can be of great use to you. You must remain ready to pick up on these hints and use it to your advantage.

If you manage to do all of the above correctly then you should be in a very good position when it comes to controlling interactions and persuasive conversations. However, there will be rare occasions when things are maybe not so civil, when things get heated and you potentially have arguments and insults to deflect. The main trick here is in keeping your head, remaining calm and rationally being able to deal with what comes your way. Perception shrinks with every uptick in emotion so suppress that fight or flight urge to respond as such. Instead try to alter the persons thought patterns with a "Disrupt and change" strategy such as misdirection back to a mundane topic or the "I agree" principle.

I thank you for choosing this book and hope you had a good time reading it. The main aim was to educate you on all aspects of persuasion from the basic principles and psychological motivators, all the way to the more advanced and complex strategies and how you can use them to your advantage.

Many of the principles I have described will seem obvious and are things that you will do naturally, which is fine as it never hurts to recap on them. However, many are not, they are counterintuitive mind tricks that require you to first understand and conceptualize before putting into practice.

Only then can you start to stack these tactics one on top of another to genuinely become the highly competent persuader it's possible to be. I have done my bit by educating you on the art of persuasion. It is now entirely up to you to put this advice into practice in your day-to-day life. Everyone you come into contact with will be trying to exert some form of influence over you whether it's conscious or not, you can't escape it. You can simple decide if you are the one doing the persuading or the one being persuaded; the choice is now up to you...

All the best!

If this book has been useful to you and you like it, I suggest you also read these my books

"How to analyze people"

"Manipulation psychology"

"Body language of people"